"I was glued to this book from cover to cover. Now, of course, I trust no one. Thanks, Belzer."
—PAULA POUNDSTONE

"Richard's deep thinking just makes the rest of us look like we're sleeping facedown in the sandbox."
—LYNNE RUSSELL, CNN

THE *TRUTH* IS IN HERE

"If the President of the United States can die of a frontal wound inflicted by a sniper shooting from behind, if UFOs can exist in the opinion of American astronauts, the testimony of the world's pilots, and the writings of virtually every culture since the beginning of time, but not in any official capacity, Elvis might be coming soon to a location near you."
—from *UFOs, JFK, and Elvis*

"A rousingly funny wake-up call for readers to question authority."
—*African Sun Times*

"A witty rant . . . Belzer throws a lot of stuff against the wall. The scary part is that some of it sticks."
—*Booklist*

# UFOs, JFK, and ELVIS

## CONSPIRACIES YOU DON'T HAVE TO BE CRAZY TO BELIEVE

## Richard Belzer

BALLANTINE BOOKS
NEW YORK

In loving memory of my father, Charles.

A Ballantine Book
Published by The Ballantine Publishing Group

www.randomhouse.com/BB/

Library of Congress Card Number:

ISBN 0-345-42918-4

Manufactured in the United States of America

Cover design and collage by Heather Kern
Cover photos of Richard Belzer by Kwaku Alston
Cover UFO photo © Bill Heinsonn/Tony Stone Images

First Edition: May 1999
First Trade Paperback Edition: May 2000

10 9 8 7 6 5 4 3 2

# Contents

Preface                                             vii
Introduction. Get a Clue, Babe . . .                  1
Prologue. The Origins of My Nightmare                 5

## PART I. JFK                                        7

1. Where Were You on November 22, 1963?              9
2. Abraham Zapruder's Day Out                        13
3. The Best Evidence Never Developed                 17
4. Umbrella Man                                      21
5. Gerald Ford and the Magic Bullet                  25
6. The Fluke of Earl                                 29
7. What the Warren Commission Found                  33
8. Hear No Evil, See No Evil, Speak No Evil          37
9. Take Cover                                        41
10. Secret Services                                  45
11. The Case Against Oswald                          49
12. The Sniper's Nest                                55
13. No Smoking Gun                                   61

14. Multiple Lone Nuts                                         67
15. Surreal Motives                                            73
16. The Usual Suspects                                         77
17. Who's Who Among the Lesser Potential Assassins             85
18. Trent for President in the Year 2000                       91
19. No Pain, No Brain                                          95
20. I Could Just Die                                           99
21. Just a Simple Nightclub Owner with a Dream                103
22. A Death Worse Than Fate                                   109
23. The Media and the Murder                                  113
24. Where Do People Get These Strange Ideas, Anyhow?          121

## PART 2. FROM DALLAS TO MARRS                               125
25. I'm Strictly a She-Male G-Man                             129
26. Anybody Up There?                                         135
27. How Ten Myths About Aliens and UFOs Equal
    One Big Lie                                               139

## PART 3. UFOS                                               151
28. What the Hell Fell?                                       153
29. Hallelujah, It's Raining Spacemen!                        161
30. Out There or Down Here?                                   165
31. What Do Extraterrestrials Want?                           171
32. The Men Who Mooned the World                              177
33. I'll See You on the Dark Side of the Moon                 181
34. Men in Black                                              187
35. Black Choppers                                            195
36. Face It . . . There's a Face on Mars                      201
37. Embrace Me, You Sweet Embraceable Anthropoid              209
38. The End of the Line                                       215

Acknowledgments                                               218
Bibliography                                                  219
Index                                                         225

# PREFACE

## Good Evening Mr. and Mrs. America
## and All the Caskets at Sea

S o what if Castro, the Mafia, or some disgruntled arm of the United States Government might have plugged the president back in 1963? As I've plugged the hardcover edition of this fine book over the past year, it has elicited more comment, reaction, and excitement than did strangely dressed men carrying shotguns down the streets of Dallas, Texas, in broad daylight the day JFK took his ill-fated ride. But then again, what doesn't?

Since the publication of this book, I've been hailed as a whistle-blower and pilloried as a paranoid. But however people react to me as a truth-seeker and assassination theorist, the evidence that President John Fitzgerald Kennedy was the victim of a conspiracy just keeps on floating to the surface.

A case in point: on June 1, 1989, the former administrator of the General Services Administration, Lawson Knott, revealed that—in February 1966—the polished bronze casket used to transport John Kennedy's body from Dallas to Washington was loaded with three eighty-pound bags of sand, drilled full of holes, and sunk nine thousand feet beneath the surface of the Atlantic Ocean. As Knott tells it, Robert Kennedy—then a U.S. Senator from New York—requested the action to offset any possibility that the casket might become an object of public curiosity. In so doing, he destroyed government property, deep-sixed an invaluable piece of evidence, and ensured that the casket would *always* be an object of public curiosity— particularly since this costly and controversial burial-at-sea could not have taken place without the approval of U.S. attorney general Nicholas Katzenbach. As usual, the U.S. government seemed only too happy to do anything it could to sweep messy assassination evidence away from the public view and into the shipping lanes.

And that isn't all. In June 1999, Russian president Boris Yeltsin hand-delivered to Bill Clinton a package of eighty documents compiled by the KGB throughout the Cold War years and recently declassified. These documents clearly refute several of the government's favorite assassination-related explanations and open the door to years of continuing speculation. Among the highlights contained within these high-level papers is indisputable proof that Lee Harvey Oswald was welcomed in Moscow like a long-lost comrade in 1959 when Americans weren't exactly on the Kremlin's A-list.

This visit took place when Oswald was just an unknown, nineteen-year-old, former Marine with a six-day visa. Despite the fact that it would be more than four years before Oswald reached the height of his importance as a government patsy, memos announcing his arrival circulated through the office of the deputy premier, the Soviet foreign minister, and the head of the KGB. They also reveal that these officials had approved plans to provide Oswald with a job, an apartment, a five thousand dollar furniture allowance, and seven hundred rubles a month in spending money. To put it in perspective, that's a deal Rula Lenska has never been offered.

American intelligence sources are still unwilling to speculate on what might have elicited such a warm reception for such a nondescript nobody. But former Secret Service director in charge of protective operations Lem Jones remarked, "People of that rank have a lot to worry about besides some kid tourist. They might have felt threatened in some way . . . What kind of threat did he pose? Or was it something else?" Was it? Gee, I don't know. Why don't you go ask Jack Ruby? Oh yeah. I forgot.

And lest the subject of JFK's brain and the botched autopsy reports has slipped your mind, you could always check the final report of the Assassination Records Review Board released in September 1998. There you will learn that, although there isn't much evidence to support a single-bullet theory, there is scads of information that suggest a cover-up, including:

- the testimony of Saundra Spencer. Spencer, who worked at the Naval Photographic Center, testified that she had developed postmortem photographs of President Kennedy. She also testified that the photos she developed were not those photos contained in the National Archives since 1966. This suggests the existence of two sets of photos.
- confirming evidence of an entry wound in the president's right temple and of a gaping, grapefruit-size hole in the back of his head. How many times do we have to hear these reports before we believe them?
- *many* personal accounts pointing to the existence of bogus autopsy photographs. Gloria Knudsen, wife of White House photographer Robert Knudsen, reported that her husband had told her and their children that four autopsy photos were missing, another had been "badly altered," and that four of five of the photographs did not represent what he had witnessed in the autopsy room. Several other witnesses told of seeing photographs in which *up to three probes* had been inserted into the president's wounds. Curiously, since three wounds of entrance would indicate a conspiracy, these photos have gone missing.
- the account of X-ray technician Jerrol Custer, who testified to the AARB that he took films of numerous fragments

imbedded in the president's neck. He also reported that he saw a large bullet fragment fall from the back when the body was lifted. Oh, and did I mention that Custer was in the process of marking his films so that he could later identify them when he was ordered to stop by a senior military officer? Well, he mentioned it. But don't take my word for it. Go to the Internet and read it for yourself.

And speaking of the Internet, the Web is also the most up-to-date source for uncensored information on current UFO sightings, alien encounters, crashes, abductions, and, of course, the latest research on all of those incredibly well-documented incidents that the government will tell you never happened, like Roswell. Are these sites legit? Judge for yourself. Visit alienzoo.com, where you'll find bulletins on the latest sightings, a great archive, coverage of recent UFO-science events, and even a message board where you can share information with other openminded people. Or go to earthfiles.com and check out the space-related headline news, dispatches on the latest animal attacks, crop circles, and mysterious floating spheres. While you're there, be sure to browse through the fascinating collection of "Real Life X-Files." With evidence like that, no wonder even a conservative Republican like Barry Goldwater became a believer!

Every time information on the JFK assassination or a new piece of UFO-related evidence is revealed, the governmentos are quick to add that they are only making these details public to put to rest the profound doubts stirred up by wacko conspiracy theorists like me. Judge for yourself: have they put your doubts to rest?

That's what I thought.

Read on.

# INTRODUCTION

## Get a Clue, Babe . . .
### JFK Was a Plot, There Are Aliens Among Us
### (No, I Don't Just Mean in New Jersey),
### and Elvis Lives!

*There are some people who still think Elvis is alive.*
—PRESIDENT GEORGE BUSH, WHEN ASKED IF THERE MIGHT HAVE
BEEN A CONSPIRACY IN THE JOHN F. KENNEDY ASSASSINATION

For thirty-five years, talking about John Kennedy's assassination has been something other than a casual endeavor for me. One reason is that on March 10, 1985, I was dropped on my head on national television by Hulk Hogan. The other has to do with quotes like the one above.

You remember George Bush, don't you? Sure you do, but probably less vividly than you recall John Kennedy, who has been dead for more than thirty-five years. But George Bush left his mark on history. He's the only American president to ever puke on another world leader. Of course, Bush was a Halcion-head at the time. In case you don't know, Halcion is a sleep medication that is banned in Great Britain but was popular in America at the time. Apparently it was decreed to be safe by our medical guardians in the FDA and AMA and was the pill of choice for an American president on an international mission. Anyway, Halcion has side effects, including the tendency to produce odd syntax problems, short-term memory loss, and erratic judgment in the user, which are all symptoms not only of the Bush presidency but of George Bush himself.

So anyway . . . somebody asks George Bush *the conspiracy question*. And make no mistake: the conspiracy question is the question of the millennium, because the very fact that it is being asked means that people have learned they cannot trust what the government has told them. So in response to this question, which is central to the way people perceive the world in which they live, Bush says smugly: "Hey—there are some people who think Elvis is still alive." In other words, he—a former president and head of the CIA—equates any serious questioning of a proven fiction, the *Warren Commission Report* on the JFK assassination, with Elvis worship. Not that there is anything wrong with Elvis worship. When Satan is busy, Elvis will do in a pinch. But all Bush and his conspiracy-suppressing cabal have offered in answer to the conspiracy question is a web of suppositions and fantastical explanations that have raised more questions about the assassination than they have answered. And with their arrogant, pat answers they have succeeded in marginalizing even the most sober critics and meticulous researchers. And that pisses me off.

At this point you might be wondering, "Hey . . . what do you care, Belz? You're living in France, sucking down second-hand Gauloise smoke. You're in bliss." But I'm not in bliss. How could I be? Three and a half decades, a twenty-six-volume report, and two useless committees after the murder of the century and this is the sum total of what we know for sure about the Kennedy assassination: (1) that the president of the United States was killed by gunfire in Dallas, Texas, and (2) two days later, his accused assassin, Lee Harvey Oswald, was shot and killed in the basement of Dallas Police Department headquarters. Everything else is a question mark. And we're not likely to get the real deal from any committee, governmental agency, or what we call the "liberal media," either. Because among the most heinous atrocities that occurred on November 22, 1963, was the twisted mandate that the government, police, and press must circle the wagons against any and all who dared doubt the official version—no matter how absurd and fantastical that version might be. The brain-damaged off-spring of that defensive strategy is the ongoing quest to make anyone who questions authority look like a babbling imbecile.

As the great writer, this country's most insightful political commentator, Gore Vidal, recently put it, "Americans have been trained by media to go into Pavlovian giggles at the mention of 'conspiracy' because for an American to believe in a conspiracy he must also believe in flying saucers or, craziest of all, that more than one person was involved in the JFK murder." I've seen it a hundred times: conspiracy research comes up in conversation and everyone within fifty paces is either reacting with jaw-dropping incredulity or giving me the elbow and asking, "You're kidding, right?"

The fact is that some of the smartest people I know, some of the men and women whose intellects and astuteness I have come to respect most, simply refuse to entertain the possibility that President Kennedy might have been murdered as the result of some kind of conspiracy or that life on other planets exists. They find it easier—and certainly more comforting—to believe that America is the only country on earth with no conspiracies at all. And maybe you do, too. That's okay. You'll do so until the day you find reason to doubt just one of the establishment's fairy tales. Then, like me, you'll begin to doubt them all. And it won't matter whether your friends are giggling or not.

Now, I'm not asking you to believe every conspiracy theory you'll find in this book. Some—like the idea that NASA never put a man on the Moon but filmed the historic "lunar landing" in the Arizona desert to scare the Soviets—may even be a little over the top. But you don't have to be crazy to believe that our government would create such a massive attempt at building up patriotic fervor. Look at Grenada. And the Gulf War. Wag the dog is what we do best.

Anyway, I didn't write this book to give you all the answers. The Warren Commission did that, and the answers were all wrong. I wrote this book to inspire you to do what the powers that be wish you wouldn't: seek out suppressed evidence . . . interpret independently everything you hear, read, and even what you see . . . question authority . . . and keep an eye out for Elvis. Because if the president of the United States can die of a frontal wound inflicted by a sniper shooting from behind, if UFOs can exist in the opinion of American astronauts, the testimony of the world's pilots, and the writings of virtually every culture since the beginning of time, but not in any official capacity, Elvis just might be showing up soon at a location near you.

# PROLOGUE

## The Origins of My Nightmare

*President Kennedy's assassination was the work of
magicians. It was a stage trick, complete with
accessories and fake mirrors, and when the curtain
fell, the actors, and even the scenery, disappeared. . . .
The plotters were correct when they guessed that
their crime would be concealed by shadows and
silences, that it would be blamed on a madman
and negligence.*

—JAMES HEPBURN, *FAREWELL AMERICA*

*I*t all began on November 22, 1963, when President
Kennedy's head exploded in broad daylight. That's pretty
nightmarish, don't you think?

Within two hours, Lee Harvey Oswald was arrested and
charged not only with shooting a police officer but with
exploding the president's head. He was tried and convicted by
the press. Then, with dozens of policemen in back of him, on
either side of him, but not in front of him (get it?), he is shot.
And instead of being put in the vehicle waiting for him and
sped to the hospital, he is "treated" by resuscitation (you
know, compression of the chest is a medical no-no for stomach wounds, but hey, he only shot the president *maybe*, but
anyway, who cares . . . he's dead!).

The whole country is in shock. First because the president's head has been exploded, and second because the guy

who supposedly did it is assassinated on so-called "live" television. NO ONE IS SAFE! NO ONE! What a nightmare! It seems like a vast mind-control experiment . . .

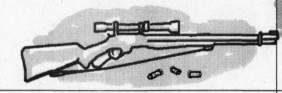

PART 1

JFK

# 1

## Where Were You on November 22, 1963?

*I* can remember where I was. And I can prove it. I have witnesses. And unlike many of the men and women who inadvertently became witnesses in Dallas that day, my witnesses are still alive.

You see, at the very moment snipers were busy making Jack Kennedy's wish come true (see quote below), I was taking aim on a grassy knoll . . . behind the gymnasium at Dean Junior College. I was in archery class and I was shooting a bow and arrow. Valerie Palucci was watching me. And I was trying to impress Valerie Palucci's breasts. The rest of Valerie didn't exist for me at that age. Nothing else existed. I always directed all of my communication skills directly to her breasts.

> *You never know what's hit you. A gunshot is the perfect way.*
> —*John Kennedy, asked how he would choose to die*

Anyway, it was my turn to shoot, and just as I was pulling the bow back the president of the student body ran out to me and said, "Belz, the president's been shot." My body tensed and I instinctively released the arrow. I'm lucky I didn't hit one of Valerie Palucci's breasts. I guess she's lucky, too.

I also missed the target. Just the same way we all missed the target about who shot JFK. Most of the country worshiped Jack the way I worshiped Valerie Palucci's breasts. They both symbolized our hopes for the future.

## FACTOID:

There were three known attempts on the life of JFK in the fall of 1963. In late October, right-wing extremist and Kennedy-hater Thomas Arthur Vallee was arrested by the Secret Service in Chicago days before a scheduled visit by Kennedy. He was discovered to have stockpiled an M-1 rifle, a handgun, and three thousand rounds of ammunition. Days later, the Secret Service received another threat: Kennedy would be ambushed in Chicago by a Cuban hit squad. The Chicago trip was hastily canceled without explanation.

On November 18, four days before the assassination in Dallas, Miami right-winger Joseph Milteer outlined the details of the upcoming Texas attempt to a police informant named William M. Somersett.

Curiously, none of these threats was ever forwarded to authorities in Dallas.

In case you have a clear memory of where you were on 11/22/63 but you're a little murky on what else happened that day, here's a clue:

The president of the United States was killed by rifle fire while riding in an open car in broad daylight. It was an event that was witnessed by hundreds but investigated by a panel of seven men, none of whom was anywhere near Dallas that day, and it was decided that Kennedy was assassinated by lone nut Lee Harvey Oswald, who was—among other things—"not an agent of the US Government." (The commission felt compelled to throw that factoid in—not that there was any reason to suspect that Oswald had links to the federal government or anything, but . . . In fact, newly released information in Oswald's "201 File" reveals that he was involved in espionage for the CIA and apparently the FBI.)

The FBI reported to the commission that Oswald fired three shots at his target. The first bullet hit the president below the shoulder and penetrated less than the distance of a finger length. The second bullet struck Governor Connally. The third bullet struck the president's head and fragmentized.

The commission, however, did not accept all the details of the FBI reports.

Oswald was later shot and killed by another lone nut, Dallas nightclub owner Jack Ruby. There was no conspiracy. Case closed. Thank you and good night.

But the case is only closed if you ignore the evidence . . .

# 2

## Abraham Zapruder's
## Day Out

*C*onsider the case of Abraham Zapruder, a New York garment center executive, out for a quiet, historic afternoon with his wife. He's got nothing to do—what does a Jew do in Dallas? Get fitted for a ten-gallon yarmulke?—so he and his wife schlep to Dealey Plaza to see the prez and glom some footage of the youthful JFK and his lovely wife who wouldn't be caught well, dead, in some tacky American schmatta.

So there's Zapruder, trying to add a little pomp and circumstance to the home movie collection so he'll finally have something to compete with cousin Myra's cruise, and what does he get for his trouble? Trouble.

Imagine, poor Zapruder, with his Bell & Howell, standing in a place every one of us has been before: the wrong place at the wrong time . . .

ZAPRUDER (who sounds a lot like Jackie Mason): *Such a beautiful day. I'm glad I've got my comfortable shoes on. Here comes the president. Jackie looks terrific. What a hat. Cut on the bias. I don't know whether to look at her or look at him. Maybe I should start filming. Boy. This is a good angle.*

Sound of gunshots.

ZAPRUDER: *What the hell was that? And what is it with the firecrackers? They see three cars and a flag and Goyim can't help themselves. They've got to shoot off firecrackers.*

Zapruder couldn't have known that the footage he was shooting with his new 8mm would turn out to be more explosive than any official evidence gathered that day. That's because Abraham Zapruder inadvertently captured twenty-six seconds of objective and incontrovertible proof that all the funny theories about lone gunmen and bizarre ballistics we've been asked to swallow are so much drek.

So what can even the dullest tools in the human shed—though not necessarily the Warren Commission—learn from this film? Among other things:

The first bullet strikes Kennedy as the motorcade is passing a stand of large trees—trees that totally obliterate any line of fire between Kennedy and Oswald's so-called "sniper's nest" in the Book Depository.

## REPORT FROM DEALEY PLAZA

If the American public had been allowed to see the Zapruder film in the hours following the assassination, the sequence of events in Dealey Plaza would have been perfectly obvious to them. They would have seen the president's head snap violently backward. They would have watched the Secret Service leap into inactivity at the first sign of the president's distress. In other words, if the Zapruder film had been aired at the time of the assassination, a mourning nation would have had the opportunity to judge the evidence—and, several months later, the stunning and unambiguous failure of the Warren Commission to explain the murder.

Consequently, the film was kept from public scrutiny for twelve years. On March 6, 1975, the Zapruder footage was passed to Geraldo Rivera by political activist Dick Gregory and conspiracy theorist Robert Grodin, who was also photographic consultant to the House Select Committee on Assassinations and technical adviser on Oliver Stone's movie *JFK*. It was aired by Rivera that night on his show, *Good Night, America*. It drew gasps from the audience and inspired reams of research.

The third shot snaps the president's head backward, explodes the back right side of his skull, and pushes him back into his seat—all obvious indications of a frontal assault and rear exit wound. Oswald, believed to have been in a building to the president's rear, would have been incapable of causing such a wound.

Even the man who became the Warren Commission's star witness, pipe fitter Howard Leslie Brennan, did not immediately act on the belief that shots were fired from the Book Depository. Although he later claimed to have actually seen a man firing from the sixth-floor window, he was not looking in that direction immediately after the shooting occurred.

A lot of other evidence stemmed from Zapruder's film. For instance, there was a question—based on the timing of the firing sequences taken from Zapruder's film—as to whether a lone gunman could fire so quickly with accuracy. Marine sharpshooters tried—and failed. Other evidence indicated that policemen on the scene instinctively turned—not toward the Book Depository, but toward Zapruder's position near the grassy knoll. In fact, Zapruder reiterated four times during his testimony that he believed shots came from behind him: on the knoll. But hey, what are we supposed to go by here . . . eyewitness testimony? That would be too obvious.

> *Of all the witnesses to the tragedy, the only unimpeachable one is the 8-mm movie camera of Abraham Zapruder.*
> —Life *magazine*

# 3

# The Best Evidence
# Never Developed

*T*here were a lot of amateur photographers and filmmakers in Dealey Plaza that day. In fact, there were almost as many photographers as there were weirdos with CIA connections. And they shot a lot of film that, oddly enough, never became part of the Warren Commission's arsenal of evidence. These Kodak moments include:

- Mary Muchmore's home movie of the final—and frontal—shot to Kennedy's head
- Orville Nix's footage, which features suspicious flashes from the grassy knoll and an image many researchers believe to be a gunman (the Warren Commission believed this figure to be a shadow of the tree branch, even though the "shadow" flees the scene in later frames)
- Robert Hughes, whose 8mm film captured movement in not only the infamous sixth-floor corner window of the Texas School Book Depository but also the window next to it. The idea that there were two shooters at the ready at the Depository—perhaps neither of them Oswald—was confirmed in a photograph taken by Norman Similas, a Canadian journalist. His print shows a rifle barrel extending over a windowsill and two figures poised above it.

## Timing Is Everything

Independent researchers have discovered compelling evidence that the Zapruder film has undergone significant doctoring. Frames have been removed, altered, and made into composites. The film speed has been tampered with in some places. And all of this took place before George Lucas!

If you're having trouble believing that the Zapruder film has been doctored by those who wish to discourage further inquiry into the JFK assassination, I suggest that you compare it to another piece of film shot by an amateur filmmaker that day.

Orville Nix, whose footage is detailed on the previous page, had set up his camera across the street from Abraham Zapruder. Since the two men filmed the exact same sequence of events in real time, the frame-by-frame succession of the two films should evolve in synch with each other. But they do not. In the Nix version, Secret Service Agent Clint Hill's movements are clearly different from the same movements depicted in the Zapruder version.

Common sense tells us that Zapruder and Nix's films should parallel each other, yet they contain two different assassination sequences. This kind of frame-by-frame comparison shows how significantly Zapruder's film has actually been doctored. It also shows you why I'd prefer to keep my home movies out of the CIA's editing room. If it were up to them, I'd be getting dropped on my head by Hulk Hogan again right about now.

But don't go by me. Two brilliant books, *Bloody Treason* by Noel Twyman and *Assassination Science*, edited by James H. Fetzer, Ph.D., totally refute any pretense that the film has not been doctored. Going Twyman and Fetzer one better, in his tour de force book, *Killing Kennedy and the Hoax of the Century,* Harrison Edward Livingstone proves that the Zapruder film is fake and discloses how various experts and scientists have corroborated the cinematic skullduggery. Better yet, see the film for yourself. Most film footage relevant to JFK has been assembled in a video titled *The Assassination Films,* from New Frontier Productions. Copies of these films are now available through numerous Internet sources. They can also be ordered through many of the catalogues listed in the back of this book.

## Everyone's a Critic

Perhaps the strangest case involving disappearing film concerns a young woman known for many years only as the "Babushka Lady."

Although the Babushka Lady was among the witnesses who were closest to the assassination scene, she was known to researchers only by the trademark triangular kerchief she wore in photographs taken that day. But her identity did not escape the authorities.

Beverly Oliver, a nineteen-year-old strip club employee, no doubt felt anonymous as she headed for Dealey Plaza on November 22 with her new Yashica movie camera. We know from photographs that she filmed continuously throughout the assassination sequence. Moreover, what she filmed was no doubt of some significance. From her vantage point, any footage Oliver would have shot would certainly have included the School Book Depository windows and the grassy knoll. Unfortunately, we can only guess at photographic evidence she captured. Her film was appropriated on the Monday following the murder by two men she believed to be Secret Service or FBI.

The men, she said, told her that they knew she had films of the Dealey Plaza ambush. They told her that her footage could prove to be useful evidence and, if she turned it over, they would return it to her within ten days. The film was never returned. Nor was any information gleaned from it mentioned in the Warren Report.

Did federal authorities seize what they considered to be a "bad film"—that is, a film detrimental to their predetermined conclusion—so they could bury it? It appears so. Did they similarly bury the Babushka Lady's identity so she could not tell her frightening tale? It's difficult to imagine any other conclusion. Could a similar approach be used to suppress other potentially harmful films—say, for instance, those featuring Pauly Shore? Unfortunately, there are some outcomes too unlikely for even me to consider.

# 4

# Umbrella Man

If the Zapruder film shows us anything, it is that there were more weirdos, gangsters, and smarmy characters assembled in Dallas at the time of the assassination than there are at Yankee Stadium on AK-47 night. Notable among these miscreants were a guy known to this day only as "Umbrella Man" and his equally suspicious dark-complected counterpart.

Even in the shoulder-to-shoulder crowd gathered on the Dealey Plaza sidewalk, Umbrella Man arouses notice immediately. In fact, he is as obvious as a circus clown in a men's room. For one thing, he is the only one who thought to bring an umbrella to an outdoor event on what was by all accounts a dazzlingly clear and warm day. For another, he performed a kind of a Gene Kelly routine with that umbrella—perhaps with a sinister twist.

 **FACTOID:**

America is a conspiracy by definition. A little thing called the American Revolution was a conspiracy. Conspiracy is as American as apple pie.

## Get the Point?

The Umbrella Man–as–shooter theory took on some credibility when researcher Robert Cutler suggested that the Umbrella Man's trademark accessory may have secreted a firing mechanism from which he could have launched a paralyzer dart at the unsuspecting president. Though the theory might seem like a jab in the dark, a completely silent umbrella/dart launcher was one of the weapons known to be in the CIA's arsenal in 1963. Some theorists also suggest that a dart armed with a paralyzing agent could have produced what they perceive to be a curious lack of motion by the president during the assassination sequence.

In photos taken before Kennedy's limousine enters the plaza, the man is shown standing casually by, his umbrella closed. But as the president's car draws nearer, a peculiar choreography begins. As Kennedy draws parallel to the man, about the time the president is hit by the first bullet, the man opens his umbrella, pumps it in the air several times, then closes and lowers it. At the same moment, his dark accomplice thrusts his right arm into the air in what many researchers believe to be a clenched-fist salute.

Was the Umbrella Man signaling to Kennedy's unseen assassins? Was he coordinating the assassination effort? Or was the Umbrella Man himself a shooter? (See box at left.) All we know for sure is what is apparent in films and still photographs: that the Umbrella Man and his companion performed their curious routine with complete calm while people nearby dived for cover or fled from the scene. Oh—and we also know this: that although the two men's behavior was peculiar enough to attract the attention of countless researchers over the years, neither of the men was detained at the time of the crime. And their actions sparked no interest at all from the Warren Commission.

Thirty-five years later, Umbrella Man's identity remains a matter for debate. Fifteen years after the assassination, a man named Louis Steven Witt was identified as the Umbrella Man and questioned. His rambling testimony—which included a statement that he disliked Kennedy and the rather far-fetched explanation that he waved his umbrella as a symbol of protest against Joseph Kennedy's sympathies for the policies of Neville Chamberlain (who always carried an umbrella . . . get it?)—has never made enough sense to satisfy thinking researchers.

# 5

# Gerald Ford and
# the Magic Bullet

> *He is so dumb*
> *that he can't fart*
> *and chew gum at*
> *the same time.*
> —*President Lyndon Johnson*
> *on Gerald Ford*

There's only one living member of the Warren Commission, and that's Gerald Ford. He's also the dumbest member of the Warren Commission. Do you think that might be a coincidence? Well, let's think about it. He's the only one left . . . and he's the dumbest one . . . hold on a second, it'll come to me.

Anyway, Gerald Ford is the dumbest member of the Warren Commission and he's also the champion of the single-bullet theory. I guess it's his fantasy. And this is my fantasy. I want to get Gerald Ford drunk one night and have him explain to me the single-bullet theory. I'd say, Gerry, can you explain the one-bullet, one-shooter theory to me? Can you explain it to the American people? And his answer would go something like this:

> *He looks and*
> *talks like he just*
> *fell off Edgar*
> *Bergen's lap.*
> —*David Steinberg on*
> *Gerald Ford*

Even John Connally believed that the assassination was carried out by more than one person, and he lived in Texas, where people shoot each other up every day, so he should know. Ballistics is an innate skill with those people. That and line dancing.

Seriously, Governor Connally knew that bullets were flying—from many directions—on November 22. Films clearly show Connally hearing a shot and reacting to it before he was hit. But if that's not proof enough for you, try some of these facts on for size:

1. There is incontrovertible photographic and medical evidence that the fatal bullet was fired from the front of the president's car. (In fact, the evidence was so compelling, some single-bullet proponents tried to explain away the president's wounds by saying that Kennedy turned to face the shooter during the attack. He never did—and the theory didn't fly.) Since Oswald could only be in one place at a time and since we are to believe that he was happily ensconced in the Book Depository behind Kennedy, a second shooter would have to have fired the final bullet.

2. Test bullets were scarred and damaged after a single shot. Despite the convoluted path theoretically traveled by the "magic bullet," the bullet identified by the Warren Commission as the projectile that passed through Connally and Kennedy was notably undamaged. In fact, according to Aubrey Bell, attending nurse at Parkland Memorial Hospital, more lead was removed from Connally's wrist than is missing from the "magic bullet."

3. The "magic bullet" would have to have been fired by a similarly "magic rifle." Experts agree that a high-precision semiautomatic weapon would be necessary to repeatedly hit a moving target from the distance of the Book Depository. Oswald's gun was not a sharpshooting weapon, but a rifle with a misaligned scope.

4. A maximum of 1.8 seconds elapsed between the moment Kennedy was first hit and the fatal shot. Since the bolt of Oswald's Mannlicher-Carcano rifle could not be operated in less than 2.3 seconds, it couldn't possibly have been the sole murder weapon.

5. Dignitaries in the president's motorcade reported that they smelled gunpowder. It is unlikely that the smell of gunpowder would travel to ground zero from the sixth-floor window of the Book Depository, a building dozens of yards away.

Is that all the evidence? Not by a long shot.

GERRY: *Yeah, uh, yeah. Lee Harvey Oswald was on second, uh . . . I mean the sixth floor of the suppositor . . . the place they keep all those books. He had a Henry Mancini rifle. He shot. The bullet went through the president, went into a diner, had a cup of coffee and a piece of pie. It left a tip, or a fragment, uh, went back into the limo and changed the station on the radio. It went into Connally, out of Connally, back into Connally, out of Connally, did the hokey-pokey, turned itself around, and lodged in Jack Ruby's ass.*

There it is, the greatest UFO of all time. It caused 27,000 wounds in two-tenths of a second. After it was all over it was found exhausted, lying on a stretcher that neither Kennedy nor Connally was brought in on.

Depending on the poll, up to 85 percent of Americans say they disbelieve the single-shooter theory.

Ninety-two percent of Americans identified Chevy Chase as the only living member of the Warren Commission.

# 6

## The Fluke of Earl

*We may never know the full story in our lifetime.*
—Earl Warren, Supreme Court Justice and Chairman
of the Warren Commission, on the assassination
of John F. Kennedy

No, I suppose not—at least not if Earl Warren can help it. But let's pretend we're presidential motorcade drivers under fire and back up a little bit.

It's immediately after the assassination and rumors of conspiracy are rampant worldwide. Always the fact finder, Lyndon Johnson is compelled to appoint a prestigious commission to "ascertain, evaluate and report the facts of the assassination," not because he is anxious to know whether the same nutcase who killed his predecessor might bump off him next but because some of the rumors actually attribute the assassination to a faction within the United States government. Can you imagine? The government killing our own people?! The audacity! Could there be anything to it? Oh, I don't know . . . why don't we ask some of those people who glow in the dark from the radiation experiments in the sixties? I bet they'll be able to shine a little light on the situation.

Anyway, to his credit, Supreme Court Justice Earl Warren at first refuses to head LBJ's investigative commission. He's got other things to do, what with the Yankees and the Cardinals in the World Series and that whole Cassius Clay/Muhammad Ali muddle (see quote below). But Johnson explains that he can't take no for an answer. He's got to dispel the idea of a conspiracy, because if there was a conspiracy the American people would think the Russians were involved, and if the American people thought that Commies were behind the death of a beloved president the resulting outrage could lead to war.

> ## Yeah, Like Your Own . . .
> *I always turn to the sports page first. . . . They record people's accomplishments; the front page, nothing but failure.*
> —Earl Warren, Chief Justice, United States Supreme Court

So he tells him, "Earl, you wouldn't want forty million dead souls on your conscience, now would you? I mean, we're talkin' voters here . . . well, most of 'em . . . most of 'em."

The fix was in. And under extreme pressure to find no conspiracy and to find it fast, Johnson and Warren assemble a crack team of investigative minds (see quote on page 31) and set about skewing the truth forever.

## The Warren Commission Hall of Shame

The members of the Warren Commission were handpicked by Lyndon Johnson, a man who was known to handpick his nose in public. LBJ was also believed by some theorists to have had a hand in the assassination itself, but don't go by me . . .

The Warren Commission as LBJ staffed it was made up of seven members. Three of them had ties to the CIA, the military elite, or worse, three were easily squelched independent thinkers, and, of course, the one remaining member was the stupidest man on earth. Along with Supreme Court Justice Earl Warren they were:

*Allen Dulles.* Dulles had been the director of the CIA for nine years until he was fired by JFK shortly after the Bay of Pigs fiasco. Though Dulles may not have had any residual good feelings for the president who made him redundant, he never met a Nazi he didn't like. He was instrumental in resettling Nazi war criminals in the United States after World War II (see page 167) and used their knowledge and experience to set up the CIA. He also worked with the Mafia on noteworthy projects such as the assassinations of world leaders.

> Great . . . You're Hired
> **Gerry Ford is a nice guy, but he played too much football with his helmet off.**
> —*President Lyndon Johnson*

*John J. McCloy* was another Nazi lover who, as the United States high commissioner in occupied Germany after World War II, generously helped to commute the sentences of many Nazi war criminals. He also lobbied against blowing up the railroad lines to the death camp at Auschwitz, Poland. Although the Warren Commission was created to "ascertain the facts of the assassination," McCloy was quoted as saying the Commission's job was to "show the world that the U.S. was not a banana republic where a government could be changed by conspiracy."

Although McCloy was front and center against conspiracy as a possible *raison d'être* behind the events of November 22, McCloy actually suggested a "Manchurian Candidate" scenario in which a programmed assassin who had been subjected to extensive brainwashing by the actual mastermind behind the murder killed the president without any conscious knowledge that he did it. This, I probably don't have to explain to you, is a curiously conspiratorial theory. Can he have it both ways? He's describing a conspiracy of conspiracies! Confusing, isn't it? That's what I thought.

**FACTOID:**

Another Successful Graduate of the Ted Kennedy Driving Academy. T. Hale Boggs was driven to the airport where he flew into eternity by none other than a young Bill Clinton.

Gerald Ford was dubbed by *Newsweek* "the CIA's best

friend in Congress." A representative from Michigan, Ford was also an FBI informant who illegally leaked information to J. Edgar Hoover about the Commission. Ford ultimately capitalized on his adamant adherence to the "single-bullet theory" and the "he-didn't-get-laid theory" (see page 75) by writing a book on Oswald.

And by the way . . . Gerald Ford has since admitted in the *New York Times* that the placement of JFK's back wound was fudged in the medical reports in order to comply with the single-bullet theory. What other secrets will be revealed?

As for the renegades, they were:

*Senator Richard Russell of Georgia.* He was the chairman of the Senate Armed Forces Committee and the head of its subcommittee on intelligence. Nevertheless, he didn't buy the "single-bullet theory" and asked that a footnote to that effect appear in the Warren Commission Report. Although the report turned out to be twenty-six volumes long, with plenty of room for a footnote, guess what Earl said? NO!

*Senator John Sherman Cooper of Kentucky* was also queered by the single-bullet theory. He said, "I, too, objected to such a conclusion; there was no evidence to show both men were hit by the same bullet."

It may have been wise to keep objections like that one to oneself. When *T. Hale Boggs,* the house majority leader and journalist Cokie Roberts's father, accused the FBI of Gestapo-like tactics (they gave him dirty files on people who questioned Commission findings), then began to publicly express doubts about the findings himself, he disappeared along with some other people and an entire airplane on a flight over Alaska, but don't go by me . . .

*Now, Here's A Novel Perspective . . .*
**We seek a free flow of information. . . . We are not afraid to entrust the American people with unpleasant facts, foreign ideas, alien philosophies, and competitive values. For a nation that is afraid to let its people judge the truth and falsehood in an open market is a nation that is afraid of its people.**
*—John F. Kennedy*

# 7

## What the Warren
## Commission Found

*T*he first thing the Warren Commission found is that it is easier to reach a predetermined decision if you overlook pesky distractions. These include unreliable witnesses who might testify to things that don't fit in with your theory (see sidebar on page 34), physical evidence that hasn't been planted, medical evidence that hasn't been altered, Mafia co-conspirators who haven't been rubbed out yet, et cetera, et cetera.

*There has never been a more subversive, conspiratorial, unpatriotic, or endangering course for the United States and the world than the attempt by the United States to hide the truth behind the murder of its recent president.*
—*Bertrand Russell, 1964*

On September 27, 1964, the Warren Commission released its report detailing what else it found. In short, it found that the shots that killed John Kennedy were fired from the sixth floor of the Texas School Book Depository building and from no other site; that the

## THE MOST USELESS INFORMATION CONTAINED IN THE WARREN COMMISSION REPORT

The Warren Commission took seven pages of testimony from Mrs. Viola Peterson, a woman who lived near Lee Oswald and his mother, Marguerite, when Lee was "a good little child" two years of age. She had not seen or heard from the Oswalds in twenty-three years. *Seven pages of testimony?!*

The Commission also brought in Professor Revilo Pendleton, a ballistics expert, to discuss an article he had written called "Marksmanship in Dallas." Together the Commission and Dr. Pendleton generated thirty-five pages of testimony proving—and I am not making this up—that Pendleton had absolutely no information to contribute to any aspect of the Commission investigation. And we're all thankful for that, aren't we?

shots that killed the president also wounded Governor John Connally, who was riding in the passenger's seat of the Kennedy limo; that there were three shots in all, all of them fired by Lee Harvey Oswald; that there was no conspiracy, domestic or international; and that there were no ties between Jack Ruby, the murderer of Oswald, and his victim. Case closed. And if you think otherwise, you're a Commie pinko who should be marginalized.

Interestingly, the one thing the Warren Commission never found was a motive.

A 4-to-3 majority of the Warren Commission went for the single-bullet theory developed by lawyer Arlen Spector and Warren Commission counsel Norman Redlich, who advocated it as the only alternative to a multishooter scenario. Clearly, the Commission's cognitive powers were limited by what it had been instructed to believe. It stretches credulity to imagine that a single bullet could wound both Kennedy and Connally, that another exploded the president's head, and that yet another missed everything, including a very large limousine, and was never found. How did a crack shot like Oswald manage to miss a full-size Lincoln limousine moving at eleven miles per hour? Or was Oswald such a marksman? Oswald's capabilities are shattered and fudged within the Commission's own documents.

*We'll probably end up with a curious situation in which most of the thinking people in the country recognize that reality is really quite different from the history the government is announcing.*

—*New Orleans district attorney and assassination researcher Jim Garrison*

Moreover, on February 28, 1964, Redlich himself said of Commission prize witness Marina Oswald, "Marina Oswald has repeatedly lied on matters that are of vital concern." But does that mean we should reopen the investigation? Ah . . . why bother?

## SOME PEOPLE WHO WERE NEVER CALLED TO TESTIFY BEFORE THE WARREN COMMISSION

•Admiral George G. Burkley, the president's personal physician, who happened to be present when JFK died. Dr. Burkley's medical statement places the president's much-disputed back wound (see page 64) at the third thoracic vertebra—thus driving another nail into the Warren Commission's coffin of absurdities.

•FBI Agents James W. Seibert and Francis X. O'Neil, who received from Naval Commander and physician J. J. Hume a mysterious "missile" that had been removed by Hume from the president's body. The "missile" was in addition to another bullet that was removed from JFK's back, specifically, 5⅜ inches below the president's collar. These missiles/bullets blow the single-bullet theory away by proving, by virtue of their existence, that more shots were fired at Kennedy than the Warren Commission wants to admit. Neither Seibert nor O'Neil appears anywhere in the Commission or police reports.

## 8

# Hear No Evil,
# See No Evil,
# Speak No Evil
## The Warren Commission Witnesses

*It's pretty heavy, huh?*
—LYNDON JOHNSON, AFTER BEING PRESENTED WITH THE
HEFTY WARREN COMMISSION REPORT BY EARL WARREN

Although the Warren Commission Report was based on the testimony of only three main witnesses, it was pretty heavy, all right. It is important to note that since its completion on September 27, 1964, an equally weighty number of pages have been devoted to the refutation of those three witnesses. This material is testimony to the dogged devotion of conspiracy researchers. It also goes to show you how easy those witnesses were to discredit.

The three witnesses the Warren Commission relied on most were Marina Oswald, who spoke little English, Helen Markham, who made little sense, and a self-proclaimed eyewitness to the shooting, Howard Brennan, who apparently could not get his stories straight.

> **We don't base our conclusion on his testimony.**
> —*the Warren Commission, abandoning former star witness Howard Brennan*

Of the three, Marina Oswald was the most tight-lipped. Even under the most repetitive and insistent questioning, she stuck to a response that should be a mainstay wherever English for Émigrés 101 is taught: "Lee good man. Lee not shoot anyone." That is, until federal authorities decided to hold her for a few weeks and threaten her with deportation. Then and only then did Marina come forth with some incriminating testimony, including some rather far-fetched stories of other assassination attempts purportedly masterminded by her husband.

> *I heard what I thought was backfire. It ran in my mind that it might be someone throwing firecrackers out of the window of the red brick building [the Book Depository], and I looked up at the building. I saw this man . . . and he was taking aim with a high-powered rifle.*
> —*Howard Brennan*

Marina's panicked babble was good news for the Warren Commission, particularly since they had located an eyewitness who was willing and able to attest to Oswald's murderous nature: pipe fitter Howard Brennan. Brennan had been eating lunch on a wall across the street from the Book Depository at the time of the shootings. He claimed to have seen Oswald take aim and fire from the sixth-floor window. He went on to say that he had such a clear view of the shooter, he even saw the assassin smirk with satisfaction after the fatal shot was fired.

But it was the testimony of Helen Markham, who claimed to have been present at the murder of Dallas police officer J. D. Tippit, that laid the foundation of the Warren Commission's case. J. D. Tippit was gunned down forty-five minutes after the assassination in Dealey Plaza. Since authorities believed that Oswald would only have killed Tippit in a desperate attempt to elude arrest for the more heinous crime, the Warren Commission was most interested in what Helen Markham had to say.

Her testimony didn't disappoint. Markham said she watched Oswald walk up to Tippit's car and speak to the policeman through the window. She also said that she had actually carried on a twenty-minute conversation with the dying policeman. (It was later proven that Tippit had died instantly from his wounds.) Jim Marrs writes that the Tippit shooting was called "the Rosetta Stone to the JFK assassination." Unfortunately, the text of the Rosetta Stone turned out to be more coherent . . . and I mean before it was decoded.

Marina Oswald has since reversed her testimony, saying that her 1963–64 statements were made under duress, that she believes John Kennedy's assassination was a conspiracy and that her husband, who worked for both the American government and the Mafia, had outlived his usefulness and was therefore silenced by Jack Ruby.

Howard Brennan, who claimed to have been able to discern a fleeting expression on the assassin's face six stories above him, was unable to identify Lee Harvey Oswald in a police lineup. Months later, on March 20, 1964, he participated in a reconstruction of the events in Dealey Plaza. On that date, he had difficulty seeing a figure—any figure—in the Book Depository window.

As for the testimony of the imaginative Helen Markham, the refutation goes on and on. Photographs show that Tippit's car windows were closed prior to the shooting. No face-to-face conversation between the patrolman and Oswald was possible. Tippit died instantaneously of his gunshot wounds. He simply didn't have time to commune with Mrs. Markham. But she apparently had time enough to place her shoes on top of the patrol car for some mysterious reason. Further, Helen Markham was also unable to pick Oswald out in a police lineup, *although she was given eight chances to do so.* She finally got it right on the ninth try. But one out of nine isn't bad.

## FACTOID:

### PLANTING SEASON

None of the bullets recovered from Tippit's body—three copper-coated Westerns and one lead Remington—was traceable to Oswald's .38 Special revolver. However, four of the cartridge cases found near the policeman were consistent with Oswald's weapon. Before the cartridges were turned over for analysis, the officer who received them as evidence carefully marked them with his initials. When, seven months later, he was shown the cartridges by the FBI, his marks were nowhere to be found. Were the cartridges evidence of Oswald's guilt, or were they conveniently planted to incriminate the designated scapegoat? What do you think? Seriously?

# 9

## Take Cover

### There's a Single Bullet Out There, and It's Taking Some Weird Bounces

When the shots rang out in Dealey Plaza, twenty sheriff's deputies immediately ran, not to the Texas School Book Depository building, but to the grassy knoll. Oddly enough, there was no doughnut residue found at that location.

But those crack lawmen weren't the only eye- and earwitnesses to the crime of the century who believed they could pinpoint the origin of the shots they saw and heard. In all, there were fifty-one witnesses who testified that the shots originated from somewhere other than the single location as concluded by the Warren Commission.

 *FACTOID:*

**WELL, WHY DIDN'T YOU JUST SAY SO?**

Ed Hoffman, a deaf mute, was the only person to come forward as an eyewitness to the assassination. He claims to have watched from the triple underpass as two men in dark suits lay in wait for the president with drawn rifles behind the fence on the grassy knoll. He also testified to having watched them fire, then casually dismantle their weapons. Hoffman tried on five separate occasions to report his observations—first to the Secret Service, then to the Dallas police, and finally to the FBI. No interpreter was ever offered to him, and his testimony was discounted.

Consider these statements from citizens who are probably more upstanding than you or I:

*. . . I heard the first shot. I thought it was a backfire. People ran toward the knoll.*
—W. W. Mabra, county bailiff

*[The shots came from] the northwest quadrant of Dealey Plaza—the area of the picket fence on the grassy knoll.*
—Robert West, county surveyor

*I saw a man fire from behind the wooden fence. I saw a puff of smoke and some sort of movement from the grassy knoll.*
—Jean Hill

*A car backfired, or so I thought. I said to my buddy, "The Secret Service is going to have a heart attack." But it wasn't a backfire. It was shots. People ran to the grassy knoll. No one seemed to look up at the Book Depository.*
—Jim Willmon, advertising salesman

*I saw blood going to the rear and left [of Kennedy]. That doesn't happen if that bullet came from the Depository.*
—Phillip Willis, retired Air Force major

*I glanced up at the Depository Building. There were two men in the corner window on the fourth or fifth floor. One man . . . held a rifle with the barrel pointed downward. I thought he was some kind of a guard. Then the president's car came by. I heard a gunshot. People were running toward the grassy knoll. In all, I heard four shots.*
—Carolyn Walther, factory worker

## Is That 100 Rounds of Ammo in Your Pocket or Are You Just Glad to See Me?

Wandering groups of men with semiautomatic weapons don't attract much attention in Texas these days. But they did in Dealey Plaza in 1963. In fact, there were so many dubious characters cruising the streets and packing heat, they had to book a second seating for dinner at Luby's.

Here is a shortlist of the most notorious.

• *Secret Service Man.* This six-foot blond in a gray business suit was seen by two (and possibly three) witnesses carrying a rifle in a gun case through the waiting crowd. He was assumed to be a Secret Service agent.

• *The Knoll Patrol.* Twenty-three-year-old Julia Ann Mercer watched as a young man in dusky-colored clothing removed a long, narrow package from the cargo bin of a pickup truck. It was obvious to her that the package contained a rifle. The man carried the package to the grassy knoll and disappeared into the crowd.

• A city resident reported seeing three men with rifles or shotguns on top of the triple underpass. Although he told his story to the FBI, there was no known investigation.

• *The Uncle Joe's Pawnshop van.* Jean Hill, a credible enough witness to be shaken down by two men who identified themselves as Secret Service, noticed a van marked "Uncle Joe's Pawnshop" parked on a short street that ran behind the grassy knoll and in front of the Depository. Noting that that street was closed to traffic, she quipped to a friend, "Do you suppose there are murderers in that van?" Similarly, A. J. Millican noticed a van advertising "Honest Joe's Pawnshop" pull up near the Book Depository. It remained until the motorcade was nearly within sight, then drove off.

*. . . I heard three shots from up toward . . . the Book
Depository Building, then immediately I heard two
more shots come from the arcade between the book-
store and the underpass, then three more shots came
from the same direction, only further back.*
—A. J. Millican, construction worker

*I heard at least five shots, and they came from differ-
ent locations. I was a combat Marine with the First
Marine Division in World War II . . . and I know
what I am talking about.*
—Sandy Speaker, building contractor

# 10

## Secret Services

*The Secret Service is under orders that
if Bush is shot, to shoot Quayle.*
—SENATOR JOHN KERRY,

  DURING THE 1988 PRESIDENTIAL CAMPAIGN

*A* decade ago, that was a joke. But can we really laugh off the possibility that passive complicity in political assassination was among the services provided by the Secret Service on 11/22/63? Researchers have compiled enough evidence to wipe the smile off anyone's face.

The November 22 *Dallas Morning News* was the Kennedy-watchers' edition. It featured a detailed map of the president's planned motorcade route. According to that map, the motorcade was supposed to take a relatively straight course through Dealey Plaza without passing the Book Depository. While the motorcade was en route, however, it unexpectedly veered from the approved route. Not only did the awkwardly twisting course change expose the president to snipers stationed at the Depository, it forced motorcade drivers to crawl along at an estimated ten miles per

> **Henry, the Secret Service told me they had taken care of everything. There's nothing to worry about.**
> —*JFK to Congressman Henry Gonzalez, on the plane to Dallas*

hour. The Secret Service would certainly have had to approve these unexplained changes.

On the whole, the new route through Dealey Plaza was more open, accessible, and, by any security agent's view, vulnerable, than the planned itinerary. Yet many sources attest that the Secret Service agents assigned to Kennedy's motorcade actually turned down an offer from the Dallas Police Department for additional security. Dallas Police Chief Jesse Curry's suggestion that he supply a car of detectives to follow the president's car was spurned. Moreover, the Secret Service themselves further diminished the president's human shield by reducing the number of motorcycle police assigned to flank the car from eight (four on each side) to four (two on each side).

**OOPS!**

In 1992, Bonar Menninger—author of *Mortal Error* (St. Martin's Press)—claimed that JFK was not killed by Secret Service neglect or even a collective hangover, but by a specific agent, namely George Hickey, who was riding in the limo behind the president's Lincoln.

According to Bonar, the klutzy Hickey was so startled by the sniper fire in Dealey Plaza that he tripped forward and accidentally discharged his own service revolver into the president's skull.

This death-by-faux-pas theory was officially disproved when Bonar Menninger was successfully sued for libel by George Hickey.

As strange as all of this seems, it cannot compare with the Service's curious behavior once the firing began. As researchers have documented, and as Jim Marrs outlines in his seminal work, *Crossfire*, photos taken at the time of the shooting show a bizarre lack of reaction from the agents riding behind Kennedy. While the president grasps his throat, Secret Service agents are looking around—two toward the rear and two toward Kennedy. With the exception of Clint Hill, an agent brought in at the last minute by the First Lady, they make no move to shield the president from further gunfire.

Most peculiar, after the first shot is fired, Kennedy's driver, Secret Service Agent William Greer, actually brings the car to a halt. Though he testified that he kept the Lincoln moving between twelve and fifteen miles per hour at all times, films clearly show the car slowing to nearly a standstill until after the fatal bullet hits its mark.

To leave a president so vulnerable is more than a casual mistake. In fact, it takes a lot of coordination and planning to not protect someone so high profile. In Fort Worth, an earlier stop on the president's itinerary, Kennedy's entourage was given virtually impenetrable protection. But the shields came down in Dallas, and JFK was rendered a barely moving target, open to attack by anybody and everybody who had it in for him.

 *FACTOID:*

### TAKE TWO OF THESE AND YOUR BOSS WILL BE GONE IN THE MORNING

*Obviously men who have been drinking until 3 A.M. are in no condition to be trigger-alert or in the best physical shape to protect anyone.*
—journalist Drew Pearson

It has been reported in *Farewell America*, among other publications, that the night before the assassination Kennedy's first line of defense were taking a few shots themselves . . . at a Fort Worth bar called the Cellar. Though the Service hasn't said much in its own defense with regard to the charges of complicity, it has vociferously opposed any suggestion that its agents were drinking on duty. Not that it matters. They drank enough just before they went on duty to fail a Breathalyzer.
Cheers!

# 11

# The Case Against Oswald

*I'm a patsy, I'm a patsy!*
—LEE HARVEY OSWALD'S CRY UPON HIS INCARCERATION
IN THE DALLAS CITY JAIL.

With the world's attention focused on the events in Dallas and a nation demanding closure in the form of a suspect in custody, the assassination of John Kennedy was clearly a case in need of a patsy. Enter Lee Harvey Oswald. Motivation: none known. Occupation: possible U.S. government agent. Last known address: on the fringes.

At the time of his arrest, Lee Harvey Oswald barely had the qualifications necessary to land a $1.25-an-hour job as an order packer at the Texas School Book Depository, but he had all of the necessary qualifications to be a prime suspect. By all standards a loser, Oswald nevertheless managed to chart a mysterious and

 **FACTOID:**

**THAT'S IT . . . YOU'RE OFF MY LIST**
The Secret Service maintained a file of the names of more than a million people who posed potential threats to JFK. Though Oswald was known to the CIA, FBI, and military intelligence, his name was not on the list.

## COINCIDENCE OR CONSPIRACY?

Was Oswald a lone nut? Or was he closely linked to some organized group of nuts we all know and love? Let's review the facts.

Here's a guy who . . .

- happened to get a job at a CIA base as a U-2 flight coordinator;
- defected to Russia with no money but somehow got along just fine;
- had no problem getting a flight to Russia even in the middle of the Cold War, when virtually no private citizens were allowed to fly to Russia;
- publicly declared—at the Russian Embassy—his intention to pass classified military information to the Soviets, yet was not arrested;
- married the niece of a Soviet intelligence official at a time when even casual conversation between Soviet citizens and westerners was discouraged;
- was summarily issued a passport back into the United States despite the fact that he had renounced his American citizenship;
- moved, along with his Russian wife and child, to New Orleans, a community infiltrated by intelligence agents;
- was immediately befriended by a former spy, established close contacts with two intelligence agents, made travel arrangements in the company of CIA agents, adopted an alias, and rented an office in a building inhabited by an anti-Castro cabal;
- got a job in Dallas working on the sixth floor of a building that just happened to overlook the president's motorcade route;
- was finally shot down in a room jam-packed with police and reporters by a mob-connected government informant.

Does this sound like a "lone nut" or someone who is entangled deep in the web of official espionage? Huh? Well? Am I the nut here? How many times does a dog have to bark outside my window before I believe there's a dog outside my window?

curious route through his short life. At seventeen he joined the Marines, where he distinguished himself as a notably poor marksman. Despite his odd penchant for making pro-Communist statements, he was granted security clearance and, according to his roommate, mother, and others, was recruited into U.S. intelligence. In 1959, he defected to the Soviet Union, renounced his American citizenship, and began living a relatively lavish lifestyle in Minsk despite the fact that he had no noticeable means of support. He met a Russian woman (who throughout her life was more than a little sketchy about the details of their love affair) and married her six weeks later. Days after the marriage, he informed her of his intention to return to the United States. His reentry to the United States raised no eyebrows, despite the fact that he had publicly threatened espionage against his home nation. He settled in New Orleans, where he hobnobbed with anti-Castro Cubans, undercover CIA agents, and Mafia operatives—but nobody really suspicious. He was known to be a passable marksman, at best, yet somehow managed to pull off an assassination one expert said was "impossible for anyone but a world-champion sharpshooter using a high-powered precision semiautomatic rifle mounted on a carriage equipped with an aim corrector and who had practiced at moving targets in similar setups."

> *There is no longer any reason to have faith in its [the Warren Commission's] picture of the Kennedy assassination. . . . Had Oswald been convicted . . . he would be entitled to a new trial today based upon the FBI and CIA cover-up.*
> —*Senator Richard Schweiker*

Oswald was hardly the ideal husband, citizen, or even disgruntled rabble-rouser, but he was a perfect suspect. He was aligned with virtually every enemy known to the State Department at the time. He had a murky identity. He was the Commie we had all been warned lurked behind every bush. (You think bushes are dangerous? Check out the knoll.) I mean, what's to like about Lee Harvey Oswald? But it was his supposed role in the shooting of J. D. Tippit that sealed his fate.

J. D. Tippit, also a rather mysterious loner—even to his police department counterparts—was found dead next to his patrol car less than one hour after and a mile removed from the mayhem in Dealey Plaza. His time of death was estimated at between 1:06 and 1:15 P.M.

Oswald, who ate lunch at the Book Depository (where his presence was verified by several witnesses), left for home early, assuming that the assassination precluded any possibility of work that afternoon. According to his landlady, he arrived at the rooming house where he lived at 1:00 P.M. While he was there, the landlady noticed a police car that had pulled up outside the house. The driver honked the horn. Oswald changed his shirt and left at 1:03.

At approximately 1:40, the Dallas police received a complaint that a suspicious man had just sneaked into a movie house half a mile from the Tippit slaying. Although cinema employees verified that Oswald had paid for his ticket, he was arrested after a short scuffle, gun in hand. The search for evidence linking him to the president's death was on.

## The Confounderance of the Evidence

You want missing links? Don't bother digging up some peat bog. Just check out the "evidence" dug up by the police that supposedly links Lee Harvey Oswald to the assassination of President John Kennedy.

MYTH: Lee Harvey Oswald was the indisputable owner of the murder weapon. At the time of his arrest, Oswald had two military identification cards in his possession: one for Lee Harvey Oswald and another signed by one Alek Hidell. The Mannlicher-Carcano rifle linked to the assassination of Kennedy had been purchased by mail order by Alek Hidell. The rifle had also been dropped off for a scope sighting by A. Hidell. The only problem is, Lee Harvey Oswald was known to be in Mexico City when the rifle was dropped off for reconfiguring.

A bullet from Oswald's gun is linked to Kennedy's wounds. Spectrographic testing of the fragments from Governor Connally's wrist were not consistent with the bullets linked to the Mannlicher-Carcano. Moreover, the telescopic sight on the Mannlicher was set for a left-handed shooter. Oswald was a rightie.

The remaining evidence was discovered in the so-called "sniper's nest." And surprise! It was found precisely where many researchers believe the police put it.

# 12

# The Sniper's Nest

*M*uch has been made of the sixth-floor corner of the Book Depository and specifically the niche designated by the police and media as Oswald's "sniper's nest." In this area, it was posited, a lone nut like Lee Harvey Oswald could put aside the overwhelming pressures of fulfilling book orders and lie comfortably in wait for any governor or leader of the free world who happened to be passing by to move into range.

But wait . . . I'm being unfair. Let me recount the scene just the way the Warren Commission envisioned it:

LEE HARVEY OSWALD (who sounds a lot like Pee Wee Herman), gazing dreamily through an open window, one elbow on a pile of boxes: *Sigh. What a beautiful day . . . unless you happen to be the president! Ha ha! Maybe I'll have a nice snack, check my little gun. Why not? Nobody's going to ask me to pack any boxes or even notice that I've been sitting here armed to the teeth all morning. Uh-oh . . . what's that in the road . . . a head? Ha ha! Here comes the motorcade! Uh-oh. That really big tree is still in the way! I should have had the old lady chop it down, but then I wouldn't be a lone assassin, would I? Aaaah-haha!*

## You Gotta Hand It to Lyndon

There was a print taken from the sniper's nest area that remained unidentified for almost thirty-five years. It would be unattributed today if not for the dogged efforts of Wallace Milam, a never-say-die researcher who could not wipe this potentially explosive evidence out of his mind. For years, Milam wallowed through the Dallas Police Department's print files, until 1993, when he finally found a match for the print. It was the palm print of a man named Malcolm Wallace, who was a confidante of LBJ's. Wallace is reputed to have murdered someone for Johnson in the 1940s, and was convicted of the murder of a golf pro who was dating LBJ's sister.

Wallace Milam . . . Malcolm Wallace! Another creepy coincidence of names of people surrounding the JFK conspiracy.

Half an hour after JFK's slaying, Dallas police discovered a nook made up of boxes that had been piled high around the easternmost sixth-floor window of the Texas School Book Depository building. It was immediately dubbed the "sniper's nest." On the floor near the window lay two carefully arranged spent shells. (A third would be found several minutes later. All of which goes to show you: your basic lone nut is even tidier than Martha Stewart!) Within minutes, the police had uncovered a rifle they immediately identified as a German Mauser that had been hidden under a rubble of books in another corner of the building. Though three deputies certainly saw the rifle, and one officer, Roger Craig, reported that he actually saw the word "Mauser" embossed on the weapon, the rifle was later re-identified as a Mannlicher-Carcano. Photographs were taken of the "sniper's nest," and the window area and suspected murder weapon were dusted for fingerprints.

Not surprisingly, the shells found near the window matched those used in a Mannlicher-Carcano, not a Mauser. And Oswald's prints were found on the boxes in the "nest" area. (He was employed as an order filler, after all, and packing boxes was an essential part of his job.) But the evidence linking Oswald to the arrangement of the sniper's nest was murky. Oswald's prints were discovered on only two of the four boxes positioned near the window. The way the prints were aligned indicated that they could very well have been left while the boxes were being packed and moved in the course of Oswald's regular duties. If the boxes had been deliberately stacked into a set formation by the assassin, wouldn't there have been more prints? Or prints indicating that each box had been picked up and carefully placed? Which leads us to the boxes themselves. Three photographs entered as evidence in the Warren Commission Report clearly show the boxes stacked three different ways near the sixth-floor window. The timing of restacking—a crucial element when considering the possibility of Oswald's guilt—is also thrown into question by photographs taken at the time of the assassination. Bystanders photographing the scene have produced prints that clearly show the boxes arranged one way before the shooting and another after the slaying.

## *The Mysterious Palm Print*

The morning after JFK's assassination, Oswald's Mannlicher-Carcano was sent to Washington to be scrutinized for fingerprints. None was found. Yet, on the morning of November 25, the fact that Oswald's palm print was found on the rifle screamed from headlines from coast to coast. Was evidence as basic as a palm print overlooked by the FBI? Or did a print suddenly materialize, much the same way as the Mauser—er, uh, Carcano—did?

The FBI statement could not be clearer: there was no palm print evident on the gun. As Bureau print expert Sebastian Latona told the Warren Commission: "We had no personal knowledge of any palm print having been developed on the rifle." At least, not at that point.

On November 26, the rifle was returned to the FBI's care. This time investigators were not only able to discern a palm

 *FACTOID:*

## THREE WEAPONS AND A FUNERAL

Charlton Heston could tell the difference between a 7.65mm German Mauser and a 6.5 mm Italian Mannlicher-Carcano even if *he* were on Halcion. Any gun nut could. Needless to say, this curious switcheroo has fueled a tremendous amount of speculation since 1963.

In fact, three photos were taken of the "murder weapon" following the shooting: one by the Dallas police, one by the Warren Commission, and one by authorities at the National Archives. All three depict different rifles! The rear bolts on two of them don't match. The wooden stocks don't match. The weapons differ in length—and even the scopes don't match. The mind reels at the real reasons for all of these obvious discrepancies, don't you think?

If you don't, try wrapping your mind around this. At 1:22 P.M., Seymour Weitzman, a deputy constable and gunshop owner, found a 7.65mm German Mauser on the sixth floor of the Texas School Book Depository. Officer Eugene Boone and Deputy Sheriff Roger Craig confirmed that the weapon was a Mauser. The following day, District Attorney Henry Wade identified the rifle as a Mauser at a press conference. The CIA, its bad self, described the weapon as—you guessed it—a Mauser as late as November 25, but at another press gathering described it as a British Enfield. That brings us back to step one: what kinds of weapons did the authorities find?

In fact, they found three guns at the Book Depository: a Mauser, a Mannlicher-Carcano, and a British Enfield rifle. As we already know, a number of eyewitnesses testified to having seen a second man in the window of the Book Depository. Did Oswald have an accomplice? Was Oswald a shooter at all? Thanks to the hit on Lee Harvey Oswald and the curiously timed death of Jack Ruby, we will never know for sure. And Americans don't like to never know for sure, for sure!

print but were able to identify it as Oswald's. But where did the print come from?

By the time of the assassination, Oswald's prints were as common at the Dallas P.D. as cattle prods. In fact, his prints had been taken three times while he was in custody. Nevertheless, as the funeral director in whose custody Oswald's body was placed told author and investigator Jim Marrs, Oswald was fingerprinted by the FBI once again—following his autopsy. Most researchers believe that the print was either transferred directly from Oswald's hand to the gun or that the print was transferred to the rifle.

No explanation for the inking of the dead was ever offered. Warren Commission adherents still consider the palm print on the Mannlicher-Carcano to be the primary link between Oswald and the gun.

# 13

## No Smoking Gun

*T*he lone-gunman theory wouldn't be what it is—which is to say, a desperate, half-cocked, shot in the dark fired off by a group of men who didn't want to waste time considering *all* the possibilities—unless we accept the notion that Lee Harvey Oswald—an average-to-poor marksman—was able to fire his weapon with deadly accuracy at a moving target within the amount of time indicated by the Zapruder film. But is this really possible? (Hey—Lee could stack boxes without leaving fingerprints! Do we expect him to be that good at everything?) There are those who want us to think so.

In his book *Case Closed: Lee Harvey Oswald and the Assassination of JFK,* Gerald Posner describes a 1975 reconstruction of the Dallas shooting that is supposed to provide us with every proof that Oswald was the lone gunman. Arranged by CBS for a television documentary, the test—according to Posner—went like this.

"Eleven volunteer marksmen took turns firing clips of three bullets at a moving target. None of them had dry runs with the

Carcano's bolt action, as Oswald had had almost daily. . . . Yet the times ranged from 4.1 seconds, almost half a second faster than what the Warren Commission thought was possible, to slightly more than six seconds, with the average being 5.6 seconds, and two out of three hits on the target."

According to Posner, not only did CBS's shooters do what Oswald was accused of doing, they did it faster! What are we supposed to learn from this?

We are supposed to learn to believe half of what we see and virtually none of what we are told, that's what! The fact is, the "volunteer marksmen" used in this test weren't exactly a random sample yanked out of some carnival shooting gallery. They were experts.

But what if the CBS shills hadn't picked off a perfect score? No chance of that! A slew of variables were skewed to put the odds on their side. For instance:

The CBS shooters did not fire from a half-open window, as Oswald theoretically did, but from a wide-open one.

Although it was widely reported that one of the CBS riflemen, Howard Donahue, scored two hits in three shots in less than six seconds, he was not able to achieve that formidable score in either his first or second attempt. In fact, none of CBS's gunmen chalked up more than one hit on a first attempt, and seven of them were unable to score two hits *at all*.

While each of the gunmen used a Carcano, none of them used Oswald's alleged Carcano. And as the FBI agent who pressed the imprint of Lee Harvey Oswald's cold, dead palm onto the barrel of the Carcano might have said: aye, there's the rub.

I'm not disputing that a marksman might have been able to fire some Carcano somewhere three times in a handful of seconds. A NASCAR driver can make a Ford go around a track at two hundred miles an hour. But jump into a getaway Pinto after holding up a 7-Eleven and you might as well drive straight to the nearest police station and turn yourself in. Where am I going with this? Pay attention.

According to Jay David, author of *The Weight of the Evidence: The Warren Report and Its Critics,* the Carcano attributed to Oswald had a problem bolt. Even Ronald Simmons, who supervised tests on the gun for the Warren Commission, reported that the bolt was so difficult to operate, three expert shooters expressed that they were unable to open it without moving the rifle off target. There was also a noticeable glitch in the trigger that required a harder pull than that needed for other weapons. Would an inexperienced rifleman and ninety-seven-pound weakling like Oswald be able to circumvent the problem? It seems unlikely.

Firing tests also put the kibosh on the possibility that Kennedy was killed with the Book Depository Carcano. When FBI ballistics pooh-bah Robert Frazier and two other marksmen conducted firing tests with the weapon, Frazier clocked in at 2.3 seconds per shot. But it is important to note that he was aiming at a stationary target some twenty-five feet away. Asked what he believed the outcome would have been if moving targets had been used, Frazier admitted, "It would have slowed down the shooting."

### *FACTOID:*

**DOWN AND DIRTY**

There is no evidence that Oswald ever purchased ammunition for the Carcano. And although the FBI found the alleged murder weapon to be clean and recently oiled when it was examined the day after the shooting, no gun-maintenance supplies were ever found in Oswald's room.

Considering the evidence, three shots fired from Oswald's gun would have been moving so slowly, the Secret Service should have been able to catch the bullets in midair.

Gerald Posner's book was so adoringly embraced by the mainstream media that it made my head spin and my stomach twirl. Especially when you consider the smug and profoundly one-sided prosecutorial nature of his massively faulty tome. Posner's "Case Closed" couldn't be more wide open. In fact, it's a grossly overstuffed suitcase—overstuffed with so many lies, falsehoods, and tenuous improbabilities that it can never be closed. Posner combines witnesses' testimony; disregards Oswald's espionage activities; refuses evidence that Zapruder's film, as well as autopsy photos and X rays, have been altered and faked; ignores key testimony about the president's wounds; has an alarming tendency to rely on thoroughly discredited and totally inaccurate statements by the Moe, Larry, and Curly of reliable witnesses, by whom I mean Howard Brennan, Marina Oswald, and Helen Markham. Posner's laughable psychobabble about Oswald's mental condition are all evidence of a mortally flawed book. The biggest flaw being his version of the back wound. The hole in the back of Kennedy's shirt was 5⅜ inches below the collar—considerably below where the Warren Commission and Gerald Posner wanted, wished, and needed it to be.

> ## Call Me Anything, But Call Me
>
> While in the Marines, Lee Harvey Oswald was called "Shitbird." The name was given to him as a testament to his poor marksmanship, but I like to think of it as a paean to male camaraderie.

Posner clearly outdoes himself in his tortured and false assertion that the discrepancy between Kennedy's back wound and where the bullet holes in his clothing appear is due to his shirt and jacket "bunching up." Posner states in a footnote that photographs taken during the motorcade show the president's jacket was "often bunched. . . ." As pointed out by Noel Twyman in *Bloody Treason,* "This statement is patently not true. At no point near or at the possible time of the occurrence of the back wound do photographs show the jacket bunched, let alone the shirt. On the contrary, photographs show the jacket was *not* bunched. . . . In fact, no one has ever produced a *single* photograph or film showing the jacket bunched. . . ."

While we're on the subject, Twyman says, "keep in mind that we are talking about a large amount of bunching" here for Posner's version to be possible—5 inches—and the shirt would have to bunch the exact same amount as the jacket; and those 5 inches of fabric in both the jacket and the shirt couldn't fold over or crease, because that would have resulted in double holes in the fabric. I don't know about you, ladies and gentlemen, but I never met an off-the-rack suitcoat and shirt that bunched like this, and JFK wasn't exactly shopping at Woolworth's for his threads.

Posner's footnote is the total argument that lone-gunman proponents use to deal with the bullet holes in Kennedy's clothing. Posner is simply repeating what others have said before, yet no one has provided a credible argument for dismissing the photographs of the bullet holes in the jacket and shirt. The conclusion is inescapable: The bullet holes in the clothing do, in fact, show the true location of the back wound. And that conclusion is buttressed by eyewitnesses' testimony. Gerald Posner's case, like that of the Warren Commission, is clearly untenable.

# 14

## Multiple Lone Nuts

*A*nyone who still finds it plausible to point the finger of guilt at Lee Harvey Oswald will be glad that he or she has eight fingers. (Thumbs are like eyewitnesses; we discount them.) Although one Oswald should be enough for anybody, there is plenty of evidence that there were many more on the loose in the weeks before the JFK assassination— and that they were doing everything in their power short of, say, shooting a president in broad daylight to attract attention.

The first person to make note of a potential Oswald double was Lee's mother, Marguerite. In June of 1960, the concerned mother appeared in Washington at the FBI's offices and announced that her son's behavior had become so uncharacteristic that she suspected the real Lee had been kid-

> There were Oswald sightings before the assassination all over the place: Oswald in Mexico . . . Oswald buying a car . . . Oswald at the rifle range . . . Oswald in the road company of *West Side Story* . . . It's the Multi-Oswald Theory. . . . It's OSWALDMANIA!!!

## How the Oswalds Measure Up

Records indicate that the Oswald who enlisted in the Marines was 5'11," Comrade Oswald, who went to Russia, was 5'6," while the dead version measured in at 5'9."

napped en route to Europe and an impostor was using his identification.

On June 3, 1960, Ms. J. Edgar Hoover herself joined the Oswald hunt, firing off a memorandum to the State Department asking for documents on Oswald and declaring: "There is a possibility that an impostor is using Oswald's birth certificate."

Whether there really were alternative Oswalds in circulation three years prior to the events in Dealey Plaza is a matter for speculation. But there is no doubt that there were several known Oswald clones actively impersonating the man who would become America's designated assassin in the months and weeks immediately preceding the assassination.

In September of 1963, while Oswald was en route to Mexico, a man who identified himself as "Leon" Oswald dropped in on Silvia Odio, an anti-Castro activist. A few days later, Odio received a curious telephone call from one of the Latins in which she quoted this comment, supposedly made by Oswald: "You Cubans have no guts—you should shoot the president."

The same month, the CIA photographed an American leaving the Russian embassy in Mexico City. The portly man who bore no resemblance to his namesake was identified as Lee Harvey Oswald. In early November, a man who called himself Lee Harvey Oswald pulled into a Dallas car lot and asked to test-drive a model. After taking the salesman on a hair-raising, eighty-mile-per-hour cruise through town, the faux Oswald commented that he'd be "coming into a lot of money soon." He also commented that he would eventually be "going back to Russia, where they treat workers like men." The real Lee didn't know how to drive.

While most "Oswalds" were as different in appearance as, say, a German Mauser and an Italian Mannlicher-Carcano, others were veritable doubles for the real thing. One Oswald was seen handing out pro-Cuban propaganda on a Dallas street,

# Take a Picture . . . It'll Last Longer

The next time you're standing in the checkout line at your favorite music shop, take a look at the photo of me that appears on the cover of the CD you're buying called *Richard Belzer—Another Lone Nut*. You see, that's my head superimposed on Lee Harvey Oswald's body. Pretty original idea, isn't it? Actually, it isn't. It's been done before . . . to Oswald himself.

Virtually every human being alive has seen the black-and-white print of Oswald known as "the backyard photo." It depicts our boy, Lee, standing in front of a fence, holding some communist tracts in one hand and a rifle in the other. I like to think of it as a sort of *American Gothic* for presidential assassins. Anyway, if the photo is one of the most famous pictures in the world, it may also be the most famous fake.

Conspiracy theorists have been pinpointing inconsistencies in the photograph for years. Photographic experts around the world have argued against the photo's credibility based on the incongruity between the shadows on Oswald's face and those on the ground. (The photographers must have been busy that day. Oswald's head appears to have been photographed at noon, but nobody got around to shooting the background until around 4 P.M.) Others have identified what appears to be a graft line where Oswald's face meets someone else's chin and other photographic anomalies. A Dallas police officer named Roscoe White stepped forward to say that he himself had fired at the president from the grassy knoll, murdered J. D. Tippit, and posed for the actual "backyard photograph" of Oswald.

There might be something to parts of White's story. In the photograph, Oswald is seen to have a prominent bump on his wrist—much like one White was known to have but Oswald did not. White also passed a backyard photo featuring Oswald in an alternate pose to his wife, Geneva, saying it might be valuable one day. She hid the photo for thirteen years before making its existence known. And in fact White did die under mysterious circumstances—in a fire, the cause of which remains unknown.

Most of all, investigators have discovered a most peculiar piece of evidence: a print of the backyard photo from which the ghostly figure of Oswald has been cut out. Imagine the assassin of your choice here! Smile. The next lone nut could be you.

while his double hobnobbed with anti-Castro agents. An Oswald clone was even photographed in the doorway of the Book Depository at the time of the Kennedy shooting while his evil twin was supposedly upstairs. He was later identified as Billy Lovejoy, who—coincidentally?—also worked at the Depository.

In brief, there were "Oswalds" sighted in Mexico, Texas, and New Orleans. There were reports of "Oswalds" buying cars, shooting guns, and changing height and appearance like some kind of *X-Files* assassin.

If the creation and positioning of multiple Oswalds seems like an unnecessarily complicated exercise, it was well worth the effort. Whatever the real Oswald was doing, the clones were busy providing him with the means and motive necessary to connect him to the murder. Oswald's blurred identity not only put the murder weapon in his hands, it provided numerous witnesses with evidence that Oswald was either a Commie or a wacko or both. It was a cinch to convict a Communist of just about any crime in 1963.

## The 60th Time Ever I Saw Your Face

Fort Worth researcher and graphic artist Jack White has been collecting and comparing hundreds of photographs identified as Oswald since the assassination. In a six-hundred-slide presentation he calls "The Framing of Lee Harvey Oswald," White splices together the images of potential Oswalds to provide photographic evidence that the facial features of each do not match up.

While most researchers are content to verify the existence of four to six faux assassins, White claims there might have been sixty or more. He also believes that Oswald's identity was hijacked by the U.S. intelligence community and used by a number of agents in the course of various acts of espionage.

Besides, it's not as though anyone went to any great lengths to find doubles who actually looked like Oswald. Some Oswalds were short and stocky. Others had faces that were shaped entirely differently. Apparently, this was open casting. Anyone—including Marilyn Monroe, Shecky Greene, and all Three Tenors—could have applied for this acting job.

## A Case of
## Mistaken Identity?

Officer Richard Rivell had been provided with a list of employees of the Book Depository. He was asked by the Dallas police for an ID on Oswald. He came back with the information almost instantly. The suspect's full name was Harvey Lee Oswald. His known address was 605 Elsbeth Street.

The only trouble was, the information Rivell provided was erroneous. And the incorrect data was listed that way in only one other place: with Military Intelligence.

It was found later that Rivell had been driving around Dallas with a man from 4th Army Military Intelligence—and MI had, in fact, tipped off police as to Oswald's address. When an intelligence agent shows up for a nice assassination-day drive in a squad car armed with a suspect's name and address, can there be any doubt that that suspect was selected prior to the crime?

# 15

## Surreal Motives

As soon as Oswald killed, well, probably *nobody*, theories about why he might have done it were rampant. Although some of these theories may seem a bit over the top, let me assure you: they are real psychobabble developed by people who were considered real authorities . . . and they are every bit as credible as all the other "evidence" accumulated against Oswald. I suggest that you commit them to memory. They can come in handy when you are called to testify before some bogus commission . . . or if you are trying to get yourself committed to some nice, placid asylum.

### Could You Repeat That So We Could Hear It?

The transcript of a secret meeting of the Warren Commission in 1964 reveals that even Gerald Ford voiced suspicion that Oswald might have been an informant for the FBI. In 1978, the House Select Committee on Assassinations followed suit, concluding that Oswald was probably in cahoots with "unknown individuals." What does that mean? I guess it means all the people he knew wore ski masks.

*The Oedipal Theory.* This theory was posited by a Warren Commission psychiatrist, Dr. Renatus Hartogs, who analyzed the troubled and delinquent Lee when he was thirteen years old. The theory hypothesizes that Oswald's repressed lust for his mother engendered overwhelming feelings of guilt in Oswald that may have caused him to shoot President Kennedy. As if this weren't enough, Dr. Hartogs went on to expound on this theory, adding that Oswald shot both the president and Dallas policeman J. D. Tippit three times—thereby leaving three lead calling cards that, according to Dr. Hartogs, represented the penis and testicles. The only problem with this idea is that Tippit was shot four times. So maybe Oswald had a wart on his equipment.

## Lee Harvey Oswald: Second-Story Man

After President Kennedy was murdered, Lee Harvey Oswald was discovered on the second floor of the Book Depository building drinking a Coke. His presence was verified by his boss, Roy Truly, and motorcycle patrolman Marrion Baker. This fact that Oswald was discovered four floors below the "sniper's nest" may not seem surprising, but just consider the timing.

According to the Warren Commission, the three men's encounter was said to have taken place ninety seconds after the shots were fired in Dealey Plaza. But Baker surely got there in as few as sixty to sixty-five seconds. (Researcher Harold Weisberg pointed out that the Warren Commission reenactments of Baker's reaction times were done at a slower speed than his actual movements, according to Baker's own testimony.) So, it would have been impossible for Oswald to have fired his gun with deadly accuracy, squeezed out of the sniper's nest, wiped off his rifle, run to the opposite end of the sixth floor, wedged the weapon between two stacks of boxes, run down four flights of stairs (actually eight short flights), bought himself a can of Coke in the employees' lunchroom, opened it, then appeared completely calm and not the least out of breath or nervous at his chance encounter with patrolman Baker and Truly.

What a man! What a suspect!

The *Oswald-Didn't-Get-Laid-So-He-Killed-Kennedy The-ory.* In brief, a sexually frustrated Oswald picks up a weapon that symbolizes his penis, sticks it in an open Book Depository window (in classic Freudian theory, a Book Depository win-dow always symbolizes a vagina; the same is not true of a port hole), and blasts away with bullets that represent . . . well, you know the drill. What you should know about this one is that it happens to be one of Gerald Ford's favorites. And Gerald Ford is an acknowledged expert on not getting laid, so he ought to know.

*The OOPS Theory.* This theory is based on the idea that Oswald was really shooting at Connally but missed. Although Oswald had even less reason to kill the Texas gover-nor than he did to assassinate the president, this was an idea suggested by a hypnotized Marina Oswald. "You are getting sleepy." What a nightmare.

*The He-Was-Just-a-Violent-Person* and *The He-Was-a-Commie Theories.* There was nothing lower than a Commie in 1963. The point is that both of these theories were simply tossed out as personal slander against Oswald so that when he was murdered on network television it could be a "feel good" moment for a grieving country.

*The Spychiatry Technofascist Theory.* You're probably asking yourself, Aren't there any conspiracy theorists who believe something *reasonable?* Like, for instance, that poor Lee had a remote, hypnotic, intracerebral control device implanted in his brain? Why, certainly there are!

## FACTOID:

### OSWALD DID NOT KILL THE PRESIDENT AS A PUBLICITY STUNT

The idea that Oswald assassinated JFK for fame or glory is not a credible motive. Blasting a world leader is a one-shot deal. Every wild-eyed madman knows that if you are committing an atroc-ity just to get your face on the evening news, you don't deny the atrocity! I mean, I know how *I* feel when I kill an audience. I'm bragging all over the place. So, come on—if you're known as a fuckup with firearms but you somehow manage to shoot the president of the United States with sharpshooter precision, and you're paraded around at a news conference, and it's your big moment and the world is watching, *what do you do?* Seize the moment by denying the charges? Hardly the smirking assassin, don't you think?

And to prove it, all you have to do is take a look at a fascinating, eye-opening book called *Were We Controlled?* by Lincoln Lawrence.

According to the Spychiatry Technofascist theory, an R.H.I.C. was implanted (I don't know by whom . . . but a lot of evidence points to Walt Disney) in the part of Oswald's brain that controls conscious and voluntary processes. When the device was activated, it stimulated certain muscles in Oswald's body that had been hypnotically programmed to trigger induced instructions: in this case, to shoot the president, then forget that he had done it. This is how some researchers—including Lincoln Lawrence—believe Oswald was used in a scheme that enriched certain international bankers who parlayed their foreknowledge of the assassination into a killing on the stock market, so to speak.

# 16

## The Usual Suspects

*I thought they'd get one of us, but Jack, after
all he's been through, never worried about it.
I thought it would be me.*

—ROBERT KENNEDY, UPON LEARNING OF

  HIS BROTHER'S DEATH

B y now you're wondering (unlike Gerry Ford), Who killed
Jack Kennedy? Maybe the real mystery is who *didn't*
kill him.

In his short years of public life, John Kennedy managed to
piss off no fewer than five of the scariest groups of guys on the
planet: the CIA, the Cubans, the KGB, the Mafia, and the
nation's billionaires and bankers. All of them had reasons to
want Kennedy dead, and all of them had the means to make
him that way. But that's where the similarity among them
ends. The memberships of these groups differ greatly from
each other, as do their particular motivations. (If you want to
get touchy-feely, you can call them a murderous mosaic.) It
can be difficult to tell these players apart
without a scorecard. That's why I have tried
to break the information I am about to present down to its essentials.

Who killed JFK? Read the dossiers
below. Then decide.

**Did the CIA
kill my brother?**
—*Robert Kennedy to CIA
Director John A. McCone*

## The CIA

Not too long ago, the CIA celebrated its fiftieth anniversary. Isn't that nice? The CIA has reached midlife. And what have they got to show for it? They took all those Nazis who had nothing to do after World War II and gave them jobs right here in the good old U.S. of A. And they might have participated in the murder of one—or more—world and local leaders! It's comforting, isn't it? Yeah, happy birthday to them. Check it out.

---

### Could Oswald Have Been an Agent for the CIA?

There is evidence that Oswald was acting on behalf of some sort of intelligence agency.

First a bit of background: Oswald was arrested on August 9, 1963, for passing out leaflets in New Orleans. His apprehension led to a scuffle, and the incident won Oswald about thirty seconds of fame on the local television news. Shortly thereafter, he was invited to speak on his own behalf on WDSU radio in New Orleans.

Lee Harvey, radio star, handled the interview nicely until he was asked how he had managed to support himself in Russia. Then he became noticeably flustered. "Well, as I, uh, well," he stammered, "I will answer that question directly, then, since you will not rest until you get the answer. I worked in Russia. I was under, uh, the protection of the uh . . . of the, uh . . . that is to say, I was under the protection of the American government. But, that is, I was at all times an American citizen."

You should also know that while Oswald was in Russia, he had in his possession a Minox spy camera not available commercially. And "microdots" were mentioned in his notebook. The CIA kept a "201 file" on Oswald indicating he was some sort of operative. Who needs James Bond when you've got Lee Harvey Oswald?

*Who:* A group of militant, right-wing American intelligence agents who believed Kennedy was soft on communism.

*Why:* Kennedy threatened to smash the CIA into a thousand pieces and scatter them to the wind. This alone gave elements within the CIA reason to want the president immobilized. But there might have been another reason for the intelligence community to take action against JFK. The CIA had invested tremendous time and effort in an attempt to secure Cuba. When Kennedy lost the country to Castro, this virulently anti-Communist faction became hostile and unruly. So they assassinated Kennedy to prevent the president from losing more ground—specifically Vietnam—to the Reds.

*How:* They set up Oswald as a patsy, coerced Ruby into acting as Oswald's "silencer," then set up the hit using their own shooters or professional hired guns borrowed from the Mafia or anti-Castro Cuban groups.

*Probability:* The CIA would encounter few problems setting up such an operation on their own turf. They could call upon sympathizers or assets among the police, Secret Service, and even the media. It would also be easy for them to tamper with or destroy evidence, deep-six potential witnesses and provide investigative groups—like the Warren Commission—with false information. Let's put it this way: CIA fingerprints are all over the events in Dealey Plaza, but there is little hard evidence linking them to the actual assassination. And that's the way they planned it. Get it?

# The Cubans

*Who:* Right-wing Cuban exiles in America.
*Who else:* Fidel Castro himself.
*Why:* In the case of the Cuban exiles, as retribution for what they believed was abandonment by the U.S. government. A small army of these exiles, sponsored by the CIA, enacted their own Bay of Pigs invasion. Kennedy had been deceived about the insurgents' motives. He therefore refused to allow the American military to give the Cubans the air cover they

## Whaddya Say We Light Up That Cuban?

He has a closet full of snazzy fatigues. He really knows how to paint a town red. So why is Fidel Castro always so darned touchy? It could be that he's holding a grudge since right after the Bay of Pigs incident when the CIA and the Mob got together and decided to try to kill him. Since 1961, these knuckleheads have tried to bump off Castro by paying his mistress to poison his food, by spritzing his radio station with hallucinogens, and even planting explosives in his cigar. Plans they considered but abandoned include hiding explosives in the shells along Castro's favorite beach, putting LSD on the mouthpiece of his SCUBA gear, and nailing him with a machine gun hidden in a movie camera. Get the picture? Then we wonder why Castro always seems irritated! Sheesh. Most people get pissed enough to kill you if you just cut them off on the highway.

needed to ensure their success. A slaughter ensued, and the exiles had the president bumped off in retaliation.

A second theory with a Cuban twist posits that Fidel Castro and his followers arranged the Kennedy murder as a response to the numerous CIA/Mafia-directed attempts on his life.

*How:* By hiring Oswald to shoot Kennedy.

*Probability:* Unlike the CIA, Castro could not have subcontracted hit men from the Mafia, because the Mafia's hired guns were trying to kill him! Nor is it likely that the Cuban exiles could execute the far-reaching conspiracy and cover-up necessary to eliminate Kennedy. In addition, there is every indication that Oswald was not the lone gunman in Dealey Plaza the day Kennedy was killed.

## The Mafia

*Who:* Men who kept wads of who-knows-what in their cheeks and who-knows-who in the trunks of their Caddies.

*Why:* The Mafia gave Jack Kennedy the business because JFK and his little brother, Attorney General Robert Kennedy, were making it their business to eliminate organized crime.

*How:* Some researchers believe they may have hired Oswald as the lone gunman; others think they con-tracted with Oswald and at least one of their own shooters.

*Probability:* Oswald had Mob links, as did Jack Ruby. And American mob-sters, who had made a killing in Cuban casinos, were furious at Kennedy for los-ing such a lucrative venue. Neverthe-less, it is difficult to associate a group that prides itself on "clean" murders with this botched-up mess. Why would an organization with so many experienced hit men on call involve a screwup like Oswald in a crime of this magnitude? How could they hope to cover up their complicity in the crime? There are too many questions here to consider a unilateral Mafia hit a realistic sce-nario.

> ### *Baloney.*
> —*J. Edgar Hoover, director of the Federal Bureau of Investigation, commenting on an FBI report documenting the existence of the Mafia, 1958*

## *The Russians*

*Who:* The KGB.

*Why:* Following the Bay of Pigs incident in 1961, the Cold War was at its height. Soviet Premier Nikita Khrushchev's vow, in 1956, that the Soviet Union would bury us was etched upon the nation's memory. There was no resistance to the idea that Khrushchev might do it one person at a time, starting with the president.

*How:* Lee Harvey Oswald had defected to the USSR, mar-ried a Commie, threatened espionage against his own country, and worked as a pro-Castro pamphleteer. It was only logical to assume that the Russians had used such a sympathetic com-rade-in-arms to kill the president.

*Probability:* It was true that Kennedy had stared the Soviets down the year before his assassination and that relations weren't exactly cordial, but the Russians had nothing to gain from the president's demise. If anything, Johnson talked even tougher when it came to the Communists than Kennedy did. Nor did the Soviets

> ### Almost . . . *Anybody can kill anybody.*
> —*Lynette "Squeaky" Fromme*

Although the media painted him as an antisocial, weirdo loner, Oswald can be linked to virtually every group that had a reason to want Kennedy dead. He was directly involved in CIA operations when he worked as a radar operator at U-2 spy plane bases. He married the niece of a Russian intelligence officer. He passed out propaganda for Fidel Castro and hung out with agents who were trying to overthrow Castro. In fact, he did everything to involve himself with the murder but dip LBJ's dog and tease J. Edgar Hoover's hair.

stand to gain anything from even the slightest whiff of possibility that they had been involved in such a plot. Killing the American leader would certainly have touched off a conflagration they were ill-equipped to fight or win. They could not be considered prime suspects.

So who gets my vote for the candidate most likely to kill a president? Look no further than the people they keep in those bulletproof glass cubicles (get it?) at the local S & L . . .

## Billionaires and Bankers

*Who:* America's billionaires, power brokers, and bankers. (What? Did you really think they were all like Mr. Drysdale?)

*Why:* Kennedy forced American steel producers to cap their prices, closed tax loopholes for the wealthy, and skimmed oil reserves, thus enraging American businessmen, billionaires, and Texas oil producers. He also angered powerful bankers by ordering the Treasury Department to crank out millions of dollars in "United States Notes," thereby circumventing the Federal Reserve. It was a maneuver that would lose the world's bankers billions of dollars over time.

*It is dangerous for a national candidate to say things people might remember.*
—Eugene McCarthy

*How:* By working in tandem with the CIA and other sympathetic agents of the government.

*Probability:* Let's think about this. J. Edgar Hoover—whom Kennedy loathed—was afraid that he might lose his job. A group of CIA agents was furious at Kennedy for what they perceived to be his softness on communism. Big business, which every day makes less compatible mergers than the one I am suggesting, is tired of hemorrhaging money. It turns for help to the CIA, an agency with both the motive and the means necessary to eliminate the shared problem and cover everybody's tracks. The next thing anybody knows, Kennedy is dead and big business is alive and well.

MUSICAL INTERLUDE: "THEORIES FROM DALLAS" (SUNG TO THE TUNE OF "PENNIES FROM HEAVEN")

Every time I dream, I dream
Theories from Dallas.
The Mafia did it, the CIA,
    the Queen . . .
Maybe Charlie Callas.

You'll find the witnesses falling
Dead on the ground.
If I were them I'd be hauling
My sweet ass out of town . . .

The Warren Commission like
    nuclear fission
Blew up in our face . . . .
Now there are Theories from Dallas
All o-ver the place!

# 17

## Who's Who Among
## the Lesser Potential
## Assassins

*R*eally, it's an honor to be included in this chapter. Okay, so maybe you're feeling a little miffed that your favorite assassin wanna-be is not up there among the prime assassination suspects with the big names like the Mafia and the CIA or those bankers, who probably bought their nomination anyway. Still, as Susan Lucci always says, it's an honor to be nominated at all, isn't it? Especially when you're in the company of knock-'em-dead also-rans like these:

*Lyndon Johnson.* Like all of you, I have a beautiful wife, a house in France, and a career in show business. You might even recognize me from the critically acclaimed and therefore doomed series *Homicide* or from one of my TV specials or perhaps my political commentary or maybe one of my personal appearances in a comedy club near you . . . twice on Friday and Saturday nights. I don't know! Just leave me alone! But anyway, like you, I would rather live my life than sit around thinking nasty thoughts like perhaps JFK was bumped off by

*I don't think that they or me or anyone else is always sure of everything that might have motivated Oswald or others [OTHERS?!?] that could have been involved. But he was quite a mysterious fellow, and he did have connections that bore examination. [WHAT?!?] And the extent of the influence of those connections on him, I think, history will deal with much more than we're able to now.*

—Lyndon Baines Johnson, from a CBS Reports *interview, 1969*

the man who would benefit most by his demise . . . specifically, his vice president, Lyndon Baines Johnson. But I wouldn't be thinking those thoughts alone.

Several recently published autobiographies describe LBJ as just the kind of power-mad, scheming, Machiavellian good ole boy who'd do just about anything to get a head . . . uh, sorry, ahead. And an affluent, Ivy League, ladies' man like John Kennedy was just the kind of guy he'd most like to do it to. LBJ's hatred for Jack Kennedy dated back to 1960 when Kennedy beat him soundly in the race for the presidential nomination. And rumor had it that the wildly popular JFK was searching for a more debonair (i.e., someone who wouldn't dream of picking up a beagle by the ears . . . a nice WASP-y retriever? Maybe . . . ) running mate to accompany him in his upcoming bid for reelection. But the clincher in the death-by-Johnson theory are the veep's curious movements as the motorcade proceeds through Dealey Plaza. According to adherents, films of the vice president's car show a Johnson so prescient, so intuitive that he actually begins to duck *before the shooting begins.* Bullets are easiest to dodge if you know they're coming, but don't go by me.

### Listen to Your Johnson

Madeline Brown, LBJ's longtime squeeze, reported that Johnson told her the Dallas massacre was ordered by "American oilmen and the CIA." She also claimed the vice president knew of it in advance.

I AM NOT
AN ASSASSI . . .
ER, CROOK

As I mentioned, until recently the only "player" whose whereabouts we didn't know on the day of Kennedy's murder was Richard Nixon. And now we know, from research, that Richard Nixon was visiting the Mob on that day, asking the Mob to help him.

I've read a lot of research on the subject. To save you the trouble of doing the same, I'm going to re-create that scene for you now. Nixon visiting the Godfather to ask for his help:

NIXON: *Please, Godfather. He's talking about getting out of Vietnam. Taxing big oil. Breaking the CIA into a thousand pieces. Then, of course, there's the Bay of Pigs fiasco, which cost you fellas a pretty penny. Now remember a while back, Ike and I asked you to whack Fidel and his brother, Raul? Well, the favor I need from you now, Godfather, is to turn those shooters around and, well, I think I've made myself perfectly clear, with all due respect.*

GODFATHER (a wad of chew in each cheek): *I know this, Little Dickie, but tell me: why didn't you come to me before? Why did you go to the CIA first? Because I know they sent you here to me. And why don't you ask for my friendship? Your wife, Pat, is godmother to my only daughter. Even if you become president, I bet you won't invite me over to the White House for coffee, or to sleep in the Lincoln Bedroom.*

NIXON: *You can blame the Jews.*

GODFATHER: *So be it. But now you come to me on the day of my daughter's wedding and you ask me to do murder. That I cannot do.*

NIXON: *But I ask only for justice.*

GODFATHER: *That is not justice. Your career is still alive.*

NIXON: *Then I ask for your friendship, Godfather.*

GODFATHER: *Good. I'll take care of this Irishman for you. I'll work it out with the CIA, the Pentagon, my old banking friends. But if I do this for you, I want something in return. I want you to spend time with your family, because you're not a real man unless you spend time with your family.*

NIXON: *Oh, thank you, Godfather. You should see the cake I baked for your daughter's wedding. It's so beautiful. The bride, the groom, the spun-sugar Cadillac with the legs sticking out of the trunk . . . all that stuff. (Prostrates himself) Can I kiss you, Godfather?*

GODFATHER: *Do I look like J. Edgar Hoover?*

*Richard Nixon.* You know where I was on November 22, 1963. You know where a lot of other people were, too. Umbrella Man. Jack Ruby. The whole cast of characters. In fact, up until recently, we knew where anybody who was anybody was on November 22, 1963—except Richard Nixon. Isn't that strange? That's because Richard Nixon simply couldn't remember whether or not he was in Dallas the day the president was killed.

Not remembering if he was in Dallas is like Emperor Hirohito saying he doesn't remember whether or not he was in Hiroshima when they dropped the A-bomb. It's like Monica Lewinsky not remembering where she was when somebody dropped a wad of Bill's on her dress.

Why the memory lapse? Because in 1959 Richard Nixon met with Howard Hughes's people and high-ranking representatives from the Mob to discuss forming a hit squad to eliminate Fidel Castro and his brother, Raul. Most researchers who accept this theory believe that Nixon's convenient memory lapse has to do with the fact that the same hit team took out the president.

Of course, where Nixon is concerned, there's always more evidence where the first bit came from. For one thing, there's the 1947 memo written by an FBI staff assistant that says that "one Jack Rubenstein of Chicago . . . is performing information services for

## Conspiracy or Coincidence?

If the assassination were a conspiracy, how could so many people keep it a secret?

Hey, just because the mainstream press won't cover it, that doesn't make it a secret! Immediately after the assassination, rumors of conspiracy were rampant worldwide. So much so that Lyndon Johnson was pressured to appoint a commission to "ascertain, evaluate and report on the facts of the assassination."

And the conspiracy buzz hasn't died down yet. Hundreds of books have been published on the subject. And even Howard Hunt would have trouble tracking down all the great (and just bizarre) conspiracy sites on the Web. But you won't. The best ones are listed in the back of this fascinating book.

the staff of Congressman Richard Nixon, Republican of California." Of course, by 1963, the Jack Rubenstein who had worked for Richard Nixon had changed his name to Jack Ruby.

*Kennedy himself.* This theory takes "blame-the victim" to an extreme. But since it's as plausible as anything the Warren Commission could come up with, it's worth a look.

Among the bits of verified information about Kennedy released since the assassination is the fact that the thirty-fifth president was suffering from Addison's disease at the time of his death. Addison's disease was, at that time, an incurable and virtually untreatable condition of the adrenal glands whose symptoms included steadily worsening fatigue, increasing weakness, gastrointestinal malaise, and, at that time, probably death. Since debilitation did not fit in with the rigorous, outdoorsy Kennedy image, it is posited, JFK ordered a group of insiders to hire a hit man and orchestrated a death that would end his suffering quickly.

This is not the easiest theory to swallow. Still, it explains certain oddities about the motorcade, including JFK's insistence that there be no "bubble top" on the Lincoln and why there were Secret Service agents dispatched to the area beside and behind the president but not in front of him (the direction from which the fatal shot was fired).

A final note: this technique has not been awarded the Hemlock Society stamp of approval.

# 18

Trent for President
in the Year 2000

Since 1840, every American president elected in a year ending in a zero has died in office. Though most people are willing to accept this curious refusal to move forward into the new decade as a fluke (there is an exception to the rule, after all: Ronald Reagan, though John Hinckley did what he could)—there are those who don't think these deaths are a coincidence. Consequently, they have been attributed to nearly everything and everybody, including numerological and/or astrological reasons, a plot by Freemasons, a Vatican power play, and a hit ordered by aliens.

Gee, Gerry, we're sorry we all

*That's typical of any presidential assassination attempt. There are still all kinds of speculation involved with the assassination of President Lincoln. It's just that the American people have a tendency to disbelieve even when all of the facts are pretty clear to those who have been involved with the investigation.*
—*Gerald Ford*

# CONSPIRACY OR COINCIDENCE?

Abraham Lincoln was elected to Congress in 1846.
John F. Kennedy was elected to Congress in 1946.
Abraham Lincoln was elected president in 1860.
John F. Kennedy was elected president in 1960.
The names Lincoln and Kennedy each contain seven letters.
Both presidents were shot on a Friday.
Both were shot in the head.
Both were killed in the presence of their wives.
Lincoln's secretary was named Kennedy.
Kennedy's secretary was named Lincoln.
Both were assassinated by southerners.
Both were succeeded by southerners.
Both successors were named Johnson.
Andrew Johnson, who succeeded Lincoln, was born in 1808.
Lyndon Johnson, who succeeded Kennedy, was born in 1908.
John Wilkes Booth, who assassinated Lincoln, was born in 1839.
Lee Harvey Oswald, who assassinated Kennedy, was born in 1939.
Both assassins were known by their three names.
Both names are composed of fifteen letters.
Booth shot Lincoln in a theater and hid in a warehouse.
Oswald (theoretically) shot Kennedy from a warehouse and hid
    in a theater.
Both presidents were concerned with civil rights.
Both assassins were involved in political conspiracies.
Booth and Oswald were both assassinated before they could be
    brought to trial.

couldn't be with you on the Warren Commission so we could
be privy to all that wonderful information only you know. But
considering that you're so enlightened and everything, you'd
think you would have known that *four people were hanged for
the assassination of Abraham Lincoln!* That's because it was a
*conspiracy*, okay? Just like this one. And that isn't the only odd
similarity between the death of Abraham Lincoln and the murder of Jack Kennedy.

## *Double Trouble*

By now you know that John
Wilkes Booth was no lone nut. (By
now you'd better be getting the
drift that there are very few real
lone nuts and the few there are
are more interested in what herbs

**FACTOID:**

A week before Lincoln was shot he
was in Monroe, Maryland.
A week before Kennedy was shot, he
was in Marilyn Monroe.

would best enhance the human head they've got simmering
on the stove than in politics.) What you probably didn't know
is that Lincoln, like Kennedy, may have been assassinated with
the approval of some high-ranking government officials—
specifically, traitors within Lincoln's own cabinet. You might
also be interested to learn that Lincoln's bodyguard—like
Kennedy's Secret Servicemen—would have done a better job
had he not been drinking, and that John Wilkes Booth, as the
preselected "patsy," was the Lee Harvey Oswald of his day. But
the most curious Lincoln/Kennedy parallel is the possible
existence of a body double in the case, proving that the existence of a killer's evil twin might be a strange twist but it is
not a new one.

In *The Lincoln Conspiracies*, authors David Balsiger and
Charles E. Sellier tell of Booth's hobbled run from Ford's The-
atre to a barn in rural Maryland. There the shooter discovers a
man who, though a few inches taller, is virtually Booth's mirror image. Conveniently, Booth's doppelgänger has a gimpy
leg, like Booth; perhaps beyond the realm of possibility, he is

named James William Boyd and he not only shares Booth's initials but he has thoughtfully had them tattooed on his arm. Though Boyd had no part in the conspiracy against Lincoln, he is murdered and misidentified as Booth. The real killer, meanwhile, limps off into the sunset.

# 19

# No Pain,
# No Brain

*O*kay. Let's do inventory. So far we've got magic bullets, bullets that don't match wounds, bullets that don't match shells, witnesses that go underground, witnesses that go six feet underground, weapons that change manufacturers, vice presidents who are so smart they duck before they hear shooting, lost evidence, planted evidence, the list goes on and on. But some of the strangest quirks in this case have to do with the president's autopsy.

Of course, I can't present all of the medical information here. I can't lift that much bullshit. If I tried they'd be doing an autopsy on me. Suffice it to say that if I ever got something really bad . . . cancer of the uvula . . . an exploded skull . . . if I were clinically *dead*, okay? . . . I'd go straight to

## Coincidence or Conspiracy?

Certainly the most qualified possible professionals would have made themselves available to autopsy the body of the martyred president. Yet Kennedy was examined by three naval doctors, none of whom was a forensic pathologist.

## And How about a Little Lipo on Those Love Handles While You're at It?

Speaking of nightmares . . . yikes! In his best-seller *Best Evidence*, researcher David Lifton argues that Kennedy's body was actually surgically altered between Parkland Hospital and Bethesda. There certainly was enough time to do some tidying of the corpus delicti. Kennedy's body, enclosed in an ornate casket, was loaded onto Air Force One, then left to languish unattended while Lyndon Johnson was sworn in as president. But naval personnel at Bethesda claim the president's body arrived at the hospital in a military body bag. Is it unthinkable that someone altered the body to conform with the premise that Kennedy's wounds were inflicted all from behind? Is anything really unthinkable in this case?

## The Pause That Refreshes

There were only two pieces of medical data admitted as evidence by the Warren Commission. They were a dental chart made for Jack Ruby's mother twenty-five years before the assassination and a detailed analysis of three of Oswald's pubic hairs. What were they looking for, evidence of fellatio? Maybe they should have brought Clarence Thomas in on the proceedings. Oswald was seen drinking a can of Coke right after the assassination. Harrison Edward Livingstone has done landmark work exposing the discrepancies and falsification of medical data in books such as *High Treason, Killing Kennedy,* and *Killing the Truth.* But hey, don't go by me . . .

Bethesda Naval Hospital. The place is like Lourdes, man. Whatever is wrong with you just vanishes. Here's what I mean.

Immediately after the shooting, Kennedy was rushed to Parkland Memorial Hospital in Dallas. Doctors there observed certain facts about his condition. They noted, for instance, a three-inch hole that had been blown in the back of the president's skull. To the doctors at Parkland and to most forensic pathologists, the hole looked to be an exit wound caused by a frontal assault. They also found a back wound below the right shoulder and a small, round hole—which they described as an entrance wound—in the front of the president's throat.

Oddly, when Kennedy's body was autopsied at Bethesda Naval Hospital, doctors described wounds that seemed entirely different. What Parkland had described as a back wound (below the right shoulder) appeared to the nonpathologists at Bethesda to be a neck wound—which makes me wonder where they wear their ties. The round throat wound was identified first as a tracheotomy—then, the next day, as an exit wound. Most curious of all, the gaping head wound moved from the back of Kennedy's head to the right front. The physicians at Bethesda therefore concluded that the president had been fatally wounded by two bullets fired from the rear, one exiting from the head and the other from the throat. The autopsy photographs were never shown to the doctors who had first attended the president in Texas. Case closed. Come and pick up your package.

## If I Only Had a Brain

Technology being what it is, it is possible that a reexamination of a critical part of the president's body—say, perhaps, his brain—might yield definitive proof about the veracity of the so-called single-bullet theory. But we'll never know. John Kennedy's brain was removed at the time of autopsy and stored in a canister at the National Archives. It would be there in perpetuity, sitting on a shelf next to Jimmy Carter's nuts, had it not conveniently gone missing in the mid-1970s.

In November 1998 it was revealed that the archive photos of JFK's brain show a different brain than was examined by doctors. One brain shows a shot from behind, the other a shot from in front. You can't have it both ways. Besides, if Oswald acted alone, why go to all the trouble of scrambling Kennedy's "brains"?

And Walt Disney wasted all that time getting frozen! He could have just gone to Bethesda for an autopsy. He'd still be alive today.

# 20

# I Could Just Die

*O*rdinarily dead men tell no tales. But the rash of bizarre, unexplained, and oddly timed deaths that eliminated a shocking number of potential witnesses to the Kennedy assassination tells a bedtime story that has given researchers and theorists a thirty-year case of insomnia.

What am I talking about? Here. Here's a list of just some of the suspicious deaths in and around the Kennedy murder. And while you read them, ask yourself this: with all this carnage, who could blame somebody for misplacing something small and insignificant, like the president's brain?

 *FACTOID:*

Most researchers concur that at least seventy-seven known witnesses to the Kennedy murder or to aspects of a plot against Kennedy died under bizarre or unexpected circumstances within years of the murder.

By the way, where did you say you were on November 22, 1963?

Just checking.

Sam Giancana was slated to testify about Mob–CIA joint projects, like political coups. He was shot while cooking sausages the night before his testimony was to begin. I know sausages are bad for you, but this is ridiculous.

Johnny Roselli, another Mob guy who was moonlighting for the CIA, was found dead and stuffed in an oil drum, with his arms and his legs chopped off. That's considered suicide where he comes from. But don't go by me.

Mary Meyer was Johnny Roselli's main squeeze and one of JFK's mistresses. She was blown away by an assailant who was shorter than she. Yet trajectories show that she was shot at a downward angle. Which means this particular murderer carried around a ladder with him for such occasions. Anyway, shortly thereafter, her diary was destroyed by the CIA. I wonder why.

Jack Ruby succumbed to a case of lung cancer that was diagnosed, oddly enough, about the same time he was granted a new trial. He died protesting that the truth of the assassination was still not known—and that he had been injected with cancer cells, a silencing technique the CIA was certainly capable of pulling off.

Just after the assassination, Dallas deputy Buddy Walthers found a slug in the grass in Dealey Plaza. He noticed that it was not the type that could have come from Oswald's gun. Rumor has it that Walthers shared his observation with anyone who'd listen . . . until he was silenced in a police shoot-out by (sound familiar?) friendly fire.

On November 20, 1963, longtime Ruby employee Rose Cheramie was pushed from a speeding car on a road that ran between New Orleans and Dallas. Hospitalized after the accident, she spent the next two days insisting that Dallas would be the site of a planned hit on JFK. She was proven right—and turned into roadkill by a hit-and-run driver for her trouble.

Lieutenant William Pitzer took the original autopsy photos of the president in Parkland Hospital. He told friends that he had been subjected to numerous grueling debriefings to help him forget a few ugly details . . . like the fact that the exit wound he had clearly seen and photographed had been turned into an entrance wound by some not-too-artistic surgeons. He was found dead with a .45 pistol in his right hand. Trouble was, he was left-handed.

But again, don't go by me. Instead, go by the numbers.

## Knocking 'Em Dead in Dallas

As Jim Marrs sums up, "the year 1977 produced a bumper crop of convenient deaths related to the JFK assassination": twenty-six in all. These deaths included the last gasps of six FBI officials who were slated to testify before the House Select Committee on Assassinations, the curious "suicide" by .20-gauge shotgun by Oswald and Bouvier family friend George DeMohrenschildt (he had apparently committed social suicide some years earlier), and the intriguing passing of the psychiatrist who ruled that Jack Ruby was sane. His cause of death was ruled "heart attack," but he took the time to write a suicide note anyway.

# 21

## Just a Simple Nightclub Owner with a Dream

*A* lot of people criticize the Dallas Police Department, but I say, Hey! Look how quickly they caught Jack Ruby! To refresh the memories of the two or three of you who can't replay in your mind the two-second sequence that made Jack Ruby famous, let me set the scene. On November 24, 1963, while the television cameras hummed, Dallas police trotted their prize criminal, Lee Harvey Oswald, through the basement of the police headquarters. A reporter steps forward and points a microphone at the suspect and shouts, "Do you have anything to say in your defense?" Immediately, Jack Ruby steps from behind his longtime friend, Dallas detective William "Blackie" Harrison, thrusts a .38-caliber

> *This young man—whether he's my son or a stranger—repeatedly declares, "I didn't do it. I didn't do it." And he's shot down. That's not the American way of life. A man is innocent until he's proven guilty.*
> —*Marguerite Oswald, on the death of her son, Lee Harvey Oswald*

## WHERE WAS JACK RUBY YOU-KNOW-WHEN?

Can you believe it? He was seen in and around Dealey Plaza by at least two witnesses, including:

Julia Ann Mercer, who identified Ruby as one of the men she had seen unloading weapons from a Ford pickup truck and heading for the grassy knoll;

Officer Tom Tilson of the Dallas Police Department, who recalls pursuing a black car away from the scene in Dealey Plaza. An occupant in that car looked a lot like the policeman's friend, Jack Ruby.

## Were the Police in on Oswald's Hit?

Evangelist Roy Rushing, who was on his way to visit Oswald, says he rode the police elevator with Jack Ruby at 9:30 A.M.—almost two hours before Ruby shot Oswald in a fit of supposedly unpremeditated grief. According to the Warren Commission, Ruby was at home at that time.

revolver into Oswald's midsection, and fires. Before the day is out, Oswald is dead. And curiously, the evidence against him begins to mount.

Ruby's explanation for the shooting was simple enough. He shot Oswald, he said, to spare Jacqueline Kennedy the pain and hardship of a trial. That explanation alone should have raised a few red flags. After all, we just don't see that kind of altruism in a cold-blooded murderer every day, do we? I mean, did Göring blast Hitler because it would have saved millions of lives? No. Did Agnew bump off Nixon to prevent the bombing of Cambodia? No. Did someone take out Bob Crane to spare the world from another unbearable season of *Hogan's Heroes*? Okay, maybe that's a bad example. My point is this: only Jack Ruby was a prince among sociopaths. And make no mistake about it, among sociopaths was where he preferred to live.

From the start, the media cryptically described Ruby as "a Dallas nightclub owner." A look at his history and connections reveals that he was much more. Jacob Leon Rubenstein began his career as an errand boy during the late 1930s for Chicago gangster

## Question:
## How Do I Get to
## the Basement of
## Dallas Police Headquarters?

## Answer:
## Practice, Practice!

Whatever else Ruby was, he was certainly a remarkable shot. Even in 1963, a stomach wound was risky business. A person who had sustained a single gunshot wound to the gut *could* live to tell about it— and about a lot of other nasty secrets, too, like who really conspired to off the president of the United States. For all his murky acquaintances, Ruby had about as much experience as a shooter as I do, and I just play a detective on TV. So how did he manage to fire off a shot that tunneled through four of Oswald's major organs (spleen, pancreas, liver, and right kidney) and ruptured two of the arteries that carried blood to his heart?

Researchers hypothesize that Ruby rehearsed the precise angle of the shot again and again before he made his television debut as Oswald's killer. As evidence, they cite Ruby's unwavering focus on his chosen target area. Film shot that day shows Ruby quietly intent on his target despite the din of policemen, reporters, and hangers-on crowded into the DPD basement. Theorists also maintain that Ruby's "training" was evident in the way he handled the .38. Instead of using his index finger to pull the trigger, Ruby fired off his shot using his third finger. One explanation for this quirk is that Ruby practiced his fatal maneuver the way a child would: using his fingers as a gun. And the NRA says that this kind of thing doesn't lead to violence in adulthood. . . .

## Here . . . Let Me Give You a Hand With That Death

As Oswald was making his way through the Dallas P.D. basement, a car was standing at the ready, waiting to take him away. Did the authorities make use of this car to transport the critically wounded Oswald to a hospital? Of course not! If they did that, he might have lived! And *talked!* So instead of letting him live, Oswald's handlers moved their breathing suspect into a police department office, where they began CPR. When they had pushed on Oswald's chest long enough to literally pump the blood out of him and there was no sign of life, they put him in the car and whisked him off to Parkland Hospital.

Al Capone. Identified as "one of our boys" by Johnny Roselli (the CIA part-timer who could have been nicknamed "Bob" after he was found legless and armless floating in an oil drum in Miami Bay), Ruby's pals included the crème de la crème of America's seamy underbelly. Dallas Mafia head Joe Civello, Giancana associates Jim Weinberg and Paul "Needle-Nose" Labriola, the infamous gangster Mickey Cohen, and a number of known hit men. As busy as a man with friends like those might be, Ruby nevertheless made time to insinuate himself into the intelligence community. In 1947, he "performed information functions" for then-Congressman Richard Nixon and was viewed by the FBI as a "potential criminal informant." He also numbered dozens of Dallas policemen, who frequented Ruby's strip club, among his allies. Oh—and he had one other acquaintance worth mentioning . . . Lee Harvey Oswald.

Evidence abounds that Oswald was no stranger to Jack Ruby. Beverly Oliver, a.k.a. the Babushka Lady, claims to have been introduced to "Lee Harvey Oswald of the CIA" by Jack Ruby in the Carousel Club less than two weeks prior to the assassination. William D. Crowe, a Kreskin-like magician and mentalist who performed at the Carousel Club, distinctly remembers Oswald as a participant in one of his acts. Four dancers in Ruby's employ recall Oswald being in the bar or even dancing with Oswald. And Jim Marrs lists in *Crossfire* four additional witnesses who have placed both Jack Ruby and

Lee Harvey Oswald at a late-night powwow with Chicago mobsters only five days prior to the events in Dealey Plaza.

It would appear that Jack Ruby was a man who was careful to cover all the bases. But was it conspiracy or coincidence that brought him to the basement of police headquarters just as the Dallas P.D.'s most important prisoner was being moved? And what were his motives beyond, of course, his sympathy for a grieving widow? Researchers have uncovered a fascinating scenario.

## He's the Patsy?
## But It's My Turn to Be the Patsy!

All indications are that Jack Ruby and Lee Harvey Oswald were fished out of the same roiling pool of bottom feeders at Patsies 'R' Us. Evidence shows us that Oswald, for whatever reason, was compelled to sacrifice himself to protect the guilty, as was Jack Ruby. It appears, however, that Ruby's reasons for doing so were far less shadowy. It is possible, in fact, to trace them straight to his bankbook.

In 1963, Jack Ruby was a desperate man. He owed an estimated $60,000 in unpaid federal taxes. He was involved in an ongoing union dispute that threatened to bankrupt his business. Though he had promised the Internal Revenue Service that he would secure a loan that would enable him to settle his debt, an FBI check of more than fifty banks turned up no trace of an application in Ruby's name. Nevertheless, the day after Kennedy's assassination, Ruby was able to deposit $7,000 in large bills in his savings account. Had his Mob buddies offered him a better deal than any legitimate financial institution could offer him? Or was he simply offered a deal he could not refuse? However the deal was struck, a man whose social circle included Sam Giancana and hundreds of Dallas cops certainly had the means, motive, and opportunity to cash in on his patsy potential.

# 22

# A Death Worse
# Than Fate
The Curious Case
of Dorothy Kilgallen

*It's a mite too simple that a chap kills the president,*
*escapes from that bother, kills a policeman,*
*eventually is apprehended under circumstances*
*defying every law of police procedure and is*
*murdered under extraordinary circumstances.*

—DOROTHY KILGALLEN, COLUMNIST,

NEW YORK *JOURNAL-AMERICAN*

Although she was regarded by most of her fans as a gossip columnist, Dorothy Kilgallen, the author of the popular New York *Journal-American* column "Voice of Broadway," was no fluff-piece hack. She was an investigative reporter with a stomach for murder cases who made a name for herself by providing a pap-saturated public with coverage of the Sam Sheppard murder trial that made people stop and think. Unfortunately, her suggestion that the truth behind the assassination of John F. Kennedy might have been buried by agents of the federal government also made J. Edgar Hoover think. Shortly thereafter, she was buried, too. But I digress.

Immediately following the assassination, it seemed that anointing Lee Harvey Oswald the nation's scapegoat, then ensuring his silence by orchestrating a televised death sentence was having the desired effect. The public was, by and

Assassination theories. Thousands of pages of theories, countertheories, over a hundred witnesses who later died of weird causes . . . bizarre accidents . . . dirty underwear . . .

Facts chasing facts chasing facts, a Japanese beetle jar . . . that jug of motor oil filled with bugs . . . a physicist's nightmare of neutrinos riding quarks in a rodeo in the fifth dimension. . . .

I sift through those pages day after day and I begin to feel like Boo Radley watching *Who's the Boss?* in Esperanto. Living my nightmare is like watching a David Lynch film of "Johnny Got His Gun" projected on rain clouds in a Tasaday village.

I was taught the truth will set you free . . . unless you want the truth about who killed JFK.

large, satisfied that the president's death had been not only solved but avenged. They returned to their normal lives feeling that the world had been made safe once again. But Dorothy Kilgallen wasn't lulled by the easy answers the federal authorities provided. In fact, she was suspicious. How did Oswald come to be murdered in plain sight while in protective custody? Was the accused assassin threatening to reveal something the rest of the world wasn't supposed to know? Who was Oswald really? Smelling a story, Kilgallen went straight to the only remaining source: Jack Ruby.

Although there could be no doubt of Ruby's guilt, the nightclub owner had consistently insisted that Kennedy's death had been the result of clashing powers rather than the act of a lone nut. Sequestered in a small room with Kilgallen, he wasted no time setting the record straight. He had not killed Oswald to spare Jacqueline Kennedy the pain of a trial, as he had claimed at the time. His lawyer, Joe Tonahill, had conveniently provided him with that fictitious story. Moreover, Ruby knew J. D. Tippit. They had spent time together at Ruby's Carousel Club a week before the assassination.

As spare as they were, these links were all Kilgallen needed to launch a full and public investigation into what she was now certain was a conspiracy. Her column became the up-to-the-minute source for stories that challenged the official version of the facts. She reported how the last-minute decision to change the motorcade's course through Dealey Plaza opened the president to attack . . . she detailed the evidence that someone other than Oswald killed J. D. Tippit . . . she published the text of Jack Ruby's top-secret Warren Commission testimony . . . and when J. Edgar Hoover threatened to investigate her, she published her feelings about that, too (see quote).

As explosive as her columns had become, Kilgallen made no secret that she was saving her most compelling details for a book she was planning to write. Those plans came to an abrupt halt on November 8, 1965, when Dorothy Kilgallen was discovered dead in her bed, a book propped in her lap, as if she had been reading. Unfortunately, the book found on the scene was a novel Kilgallen had already finished and the reading glasses she needed desperately were nowhere to be found. The cause of her death was listed alternately as heart attack or accidental barbiturate poisoning. The incriminating file she had so painstakingly assembled was never discovered.

> *I would be inclined to believe that the FBI might have been more profitably employed in probing the facts of the [Kennedy] case rather than how I got them.*
> —*Dorothy Kilgallen*

# 23

# The Media and
# the Murder

*. . . and that's the way I SAY it was . . .*
*Any questions? Huh? Who killed JFK?*
*Whoops! Look at that. We're out of time!*
—THE MOST TRUSTED MAN IN AMERICA,
    TELLING THE WAY IT *REALLY* IS

W hat is it that makes human beings believe one fact over another? Information, verification, believ-ability. These are the tools we use to make informed decisions. But what if we couldn't trust the information we got from our news-

> ***One journalist***
> ***is worth twenty***
> ***agents.***
> *—unnamed CIA official*
> *to Carl Bernstein*

papers, newscasts, and history books? And what if we couldn't believe the sources we rely on every day? Well, guess what, folks . . . the truth is we really *can't* trust most if not all sources of information. Why, you ask? Why? I'll tell you why. Because the media has been infiltrated by the CIA.

I know, I know. I could tell you that and you'd think, Yeah, well . . . could be. Instead I tell you that the CIA determines much of what we know—and most important, what we get not to know—and you're thinking, Wow—poor Richard. He must have an undiagnosed case of Belzheimer's disease. But the sad fact is I'm all there. Worse yet, the CIA is all there—at 30 Rock, at CNN headquarters in Atlanta, and everywhere else news is broadcast, written, or edited. Here's how I know.

## No News Is Good News

Some of the stories that have intrigued conspiracy researchers most were like JFK: they appeared in public once too often, were killed, were buried, and were never heard of again. Until now.

Here is a selection of my favorite vanishing news stories. To save the CIA from having to infiltrate book publishing (like they haven't . . . ), read fast, white them out, then drink a can of Sterno. You won't remember a thing.

Among some of the more disturbing stories that were curiously uncovered or heavily censored by whomever (just pick the appropriate government agency)—nuclear proliferation in space; the government's high-tech ability to spy on its own citizens; aspects of the Gulf War; agribusinesses' attempts to thwart their responsibility in food safety; government involvement in drug trafficking; environmental protection policies' lack of protection; our true Chinese connections; how toxic waste is handled; U.S. covert operations throughout the world; and many official stories not generally known. If you seek to be further informed on how much you're not being informed, then I urge you to acquire the Project Censored Yearbooks—an annual compendium of "the news that didn't make the news and why."

In 1977 Carl Bernstein, the journalist who uncovered the illegal break-in at the Watergate Apartments in 1972, reported in *Rolling Stone* magazine that more than four hundred American print and television journalists had secretly acted as operatives or agents for the CIA. Furthermore, to the shock of both ends of the political spectrum—those who view with scorn or look with hope to a "liberal media"—Bernstein pointed the finger specifically at the *New York Times,* labeling the paper one of the CIA's most reliable mouthpieces. The *Times* immediately leaped to its own defense. Sort of. In a printed response, the

*Times* editorial board amended Bernstein's count, saying that in actuality there were "more than 800 news and public information organizations and individuals" allied with the CIA. Consequently, they were responsible for only a small percentage of CIA-sponsored news.

Whew! What a relief! Here I was thinking that the *New York Times,* one of the most trusted sources of information in the world, had gotten on its knees for the CIA. But in actuality, the

---

### Conspiracy or Coincidence? The Persecution of Oliver Stone

In October 1998, the FBI announced that it was releasing nearly 100,000 pages of never-before-seen documents relating to the assassination of John Kennedy. Do you recall seeing that announcement in the paper? Can you call to mind any new information you learned from the documents the FBI released? Of course you can't. That's because the print and broadcast media decided that in nearly 100,000 pages of new material there was nothing worth reporting. And you know what? They're right. The release of these documents is a sham—just another media ploy to convince a skeptical America that the government has at last come clean about JFK's death.

If only Oliver Stone's *JFK* had gotten the same treatment—or even fair treatment—from the so-called "liberal media." The media had plenty to say long before Stone's film was even released. Print journalists went on record with attacks so vicious and reviews so dire that it began to appear—to truly impartial sources—that Stone was being lynched in print. Stone himself believes he became a target because his film dares to suggest that the press missed the true story behind the crime of the century. But what do I know? I just read too many newspapers.

## What's the
## Conspiracy, Kenneth?

Over the years, CBS anchorman Dan Rather has done just about everything to get us to trust him. He delivered the news standing up. He delivered the news with a female co-anchor. He delivered the news wearing a sweater like Mr. Rogers. But he never tried the most obvious way to get the American public to trust him: quitting the CIA.

I'm not sure when Dan Rather became a G-man. What I do know is that he became the darling of the conspiracy theorists shortly after the shooting in Dealey Plaza. Despite the fact that there were hundreds of journalists at work at the time of the shooting, Dan Rather was chosen to be the first media representative to see the Zapruder film. Like any good newsman, he hightailed it to the cameras to report what he saw. And what he saw was the president's head driven violently forward. FORWARD? Did you say forward, Richard? Yes, I did. But that's no reason for all of you rabidly pro-single-shooter people out there to start foaming. Dan Rather may have been shown the first known doctored version of the Zapruder film. I mean, who better to show it to than a CIA-connected talking head? But curiously, Rather never repeated the details of what must have been a vivid memory. The story simply vanished.

I know what you're thinking. You're thinking, Richard—you can't go around accusing every television personality with plastic surgery as obvious as a circus clown in a men's room of being a CIA asset. Fine. But Dan's story isn't as superficial as his broadcasting.

entire information machine—from the most respected figureheads to the lowliest reporters in Bumfuck, Nowhere—are feeding the Feds their notes, making connections for the CIA, sharing their sources, and who-knows-what-else. It's like finding out that your wife has been sleeping with your best friend. Then having her tell you, Hey—don't sweat it. I've also been sleeping with your best friend's father, your best friend's

According to researcher John Judge, there is a list in the custody of the Federal Emergency Management Agency that itemizes every American considered to be crucial to this nation's survival. In case of a national emergency, those individuals whose names appear on the list are to be transported immediately to safe haven, where they will remain until the crisis passes. (If you're wondering where you will be until the crisis passes, just bend over and stick your head as far as you can between your legs. You'll be kissing your ass good-bye.) Anyway, guess who's on the list? Dan Rather. Don't get me wrong—I can see saving certain people, like Thomas Noguchi so he can get a start on all those autopsies, or Richard Simmons so the survivors don't all get flabby and out of shape. But Dan Rather? For what? So he could go on the news and say, "Well, there was a nuclear war, but don't worry about it. . . . I'm okay!"

But if you're still not convinced that the man has connections, consider this: On February 20, 1998, the United States was talking tough with Iraq. As you might recall, Iraq was refusing to allow UN inspectors inside their factories lest the inspectors discover the stockpile of weapons we all know is there. Anyway, it appeared that the United States and Iraq were dangerously close to war. Except to those Americans lucky enough to be getting a certain live feed from CBS news. To them it appeared that the war had already begun.

For about twenty minutes, CBS broadcast an embarrassing story detailing the escalating "Iraq–U.S. conflict." Wearing his most somber expression, Rather described the bombing that, he assured us, had commenced, adding at one point that the number of casualties of the conflict could not yet be ascertained. Though no war erupted, Rather went on and on, the Chromakey behind him, blithely rehearsing a report of breaking news that would, in reality, never break. Though CBS shrugged the incident off, claiming the anchor was simply testing new music and graphics, the story confirms suspicion that there is a strong link between the Pentagon—which relies on media-generated propaganda to muster public support during wartime—CBS, and Dan Rather.

mechanic, your best friend's proctologist, and your best friend's dog. Your best friend doesn't mean a thing to me.

Like you, I'm a Jew who plays a detective on a television drama. Also like you, I read six newspapers every day. I am still hoping that one day one of them might give me something other than all the news the CIA thinks is fit to print. Fat chance. As Jonathan Vankin and John Whalen demonstrate in their conspiracy classic, *The 60 Greatest Conspiracies of All Time,* the list of distinguished publishers and journalists known to have done the nasty with the CIA includes generations of journalism's A-list. Former *New York Times* publisher Arthur Hays Sulzberger, CBS president William Paley, and magazine mogul Henry Luce did everything they could—including loan out their employees—to placate the CIA. According to Vankin and Whalen, known agents and assets are in place at ABC, CBS, and NBC, as well as "the Associated Press, United Press International, Reuters, *Newsweek* magazine, Scripps-Howard, Hearst newspapers, and the *Miami Herald*." That's why a news-hungry world knows all about the distinguishing characteristics of the president's penis (remember that map of Russia on Gorbachev's head? Well, Clinton's got the White House internship application on the organ *he* thinks with) but almost nothing about the murder in broad daylight of the leader of the free world.

This is not to say that the media has been totally silent on the issue of JFK. There were some responsible members of the press. Otherwise we would never have seen headlines like these:

## Inside the CIA's Drug Lab
*As a reporter, and I don't want to say that's the only context, I've tried everything. I can say, too, with confidence I know a fair amount about LSD. I've never been a social user of any of these things, but my curiosity has carried me into a lot of interesting areas. As an example, in 1955 or '56, I had someone in the Houston police station shoot me up with heroin so I could do a story about it. I came out understanding full well how one could be addicted to "smack" and quickly.*
—Dan Rather,
Ladies' Home Journal, *1980*

## JFK REINCARNATED AS 7-YEAR-OLD BOY

Young boy wants to overthrow Castro. Sneaks a bevy of girlfriends into his treehouse. Just like JFK! Simply astounding.

## JFK ALIVE IN SWISS ALPS

So that's where he's been! I feel so bad. I haven't really been in touch for . . . oh, thirty-five years. I know. I'll pick up a Hallmark card. Hallmark has something for every occasion. I'll look in the "Sorry to Hear You've Come Down with an Assassination" section. While I'm there, I'll pick one up for Lee Harvey Oswald, too.

## KENNEDY BUGGED JACKIE'S BRA

Oh, here's an insight: Jackie did it because JFK bugged her bra. Honey, could you speak into my cleavage, please? This is for posterity.

## OSWALD MAKES BLACKWELL'S WORST-DRESSED LIST

What becomes a lone nut most? A zoot suit and fedora? Then maybe he should have had his head superimposed on Frank Sinatra's body. Hey, it worked for Harry Connick, Jr.

# 24

# Where Do People Get
# These Strange Ideas,
# Anyhow?

> **This book is so far
> removed from reality
> that it cannot pretend
> to represent what
> really happened in
> Dallas that day.**
> —*pro–Warren Commission theorist
> Jim Moore, criticizing a book
> called* High Treason *by
> Robert J. Groden and Harrison
> Livingstone. In it Groden and
> Livingstone assert that the
> president's autopsy photos
> were altered and that the CIA is
> responsible for a massive cover-
> up of evidence in the case.*

Where, oh where? I know . . . the idea that surgeons may have done more doctoring to Kennedy's autopsy reports than they did on their temporarily living patients or that the president just might have been offed by somebody we know and love (or, in Lyndon Johnson's case, just *know*) can seem a little extreme. . . . Better to take a few minutes to relax, maybe look at the paper. Take your mind off all of that paranoid thinking.

But wait a minute . . . what's this?

NEWS FLASH! Not that we've been hiding anything for the last thirty-five years, but . . . we just discovered that the records of the autopsy performed on John F. Kennedy are, oddly enough, incomplete! According to the Assassination Records Review Board, August 3, 1998, Dr. James Humes revealed—under oath and after what is described as "persistent questioning"—that he chucked both the notes he had taken during Kennedy's autopsy at Bethesda Naval Hospital and his first draft of the autopsy report into the fireplace at his home. Why? All together now: to protect "the privacy and the sensibilities of the president's family!" Why else?

The board also noted that "there have been shortcomings that led many to question not only the completeness of the autopsy records but the lack of a prompt and complete analysis of the records by the Warren Commission." But that era of suspicion and distrust is behind us now. I feel better now that Jack Ruby and a Navy doctor are giving the same lame excuse for obstructing justice in a murder case of unparalleled historical significance. How about you?

NEWS FLASH! On July 31, 1998, the Assassination Records Review Board released testimony indicating that they have evidence of the existence of a second set of autopsy photos—and that these photos were taken in addition to the set now housed at the National Archives. The photographs were never made public, and their whereabouts are unknown.

The photos were documented in 1997 by Saundra Spencer, whose job, in 1963, included developing photos at the Naval Photographic Center. She asserted that the photos housed at the archives were not the photos she developed. Those she worked with showed "no blood or opening cavities."

Speculating on the reason for the discrepancy, Ms. Spencer suggested that the second set of photographs were taken of a cleaned-up corpse at the request of the Kennedy family. The family, she surmised, might have retained the sanitized set in case autopsy photographs had to be made available to a squeamish public during the course of an investigation.

Of course, as it turned out, there was very little chance of that.

NEWS FLASH! On August 9, 1998, the Secret Service released the results of their long-term study "Preventing Assassinations." In it, they debunk the stereotypical image of the assassin as a disenfranchised, pathetic loner or even as a swaggering, shotgun-wielding, pinko lawn-jockey with someone else's head superimposed on his shoulders.

> # *FACTOID:*
>
> ### EEEWWWW . . . WHO LOOKS AT THAT DISGUSTING STUFF, ANYWAY?
>
> I can assure you that everybody on the Internet with a screen name like "Mauser" or "Marilyn44DD" has seen the autopsy photos. The same cannot be said for anyone who served on the Warren Commission. Curiously, the panel chose not to view either the Kennedy autopsy X rays or the photographs.

In this in-depth study of eighty-three American politician and celebrity stalkers, Secret Service researchers and psychoanalysts describe the typical assassin as white, perhaps a college graduate, who had never been arrested as an adult for a violent offense. In addition, the assassin almost always appears to be mentally stable and does what he does to put himself in proximity to fame.

So what is the Secret Service saying here . . . that an assassin could act and look a lot like your basic Secret Service agent? It seems to me it is. But like I said, don't go by me.

## Last, but Not Least

Well, there you have it: my obsessive reweaving of a story that began more than three decades ago. It is a story that has more plot lines—some leading to the heart of the matter, others seemingly nowhere at all—than J. Edgar had feather boas. It is also a story that has yet to be provided with a credible ending.

No doubt you're wondering how what I have described here could be possible. How could a nation's future be washed away by a tidal wave of corruption? That, I know, is how it seems. But, as I have come to understand the events at Dealey Plaza, John Kennedy wasn't swallowed up by a single, precisely orchestrated, overwhelming evil. He was undone by a motley group of gain-seekers—including common thugs, elements of the CIA and the FBI and the MIA, organized-crime figures, media shills, a strip-joint owner, and dozens of other people who wouldn't have thought to sit near each other at an assassins' picnic—who somehow came together, knowingly or unknowingly, to effectively bring about a bloody coup in broad daylight in the Land of the Free. In other words, this kind of party isn't planned; this kind of party just "happens."

> *Sometimes in the dark of night I begin to think. And I wonder if Lee started all of this violence.*
> —Marina Oswald

But if it happened once, can it happen again? Don't panic. It could only happen in a country where:

- certain government functionaries maintain secret files on their own citizens and leaders;
- the media reports what they feel we ought to hear rather than the facts;
- matters of national interest are investigated by a group of politicians, which is more concerned with maintaining the status quo than arriving at the truth;
- political leaders are subject to scandal, accusation, and blackmail—and their families are compelled to acquiesce to a cover-up in order to maintain their dignity; and
- political extremists will resort to murder to achieve an end.

In other words, what do you have planned for next week? Maybe you should pencil in some time for a conspiracy or two. I've got a sense about these things, you know.

If, like Marina, you're still wondering who started all of this violence, there are plenty of avenues to search. Check out the bibliography at the back of this book. This is only the beginning.

# PART 2

# From Dallas to Marrs

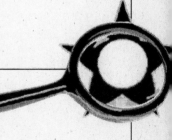

*f* I have accomplished what I set out to do in the first part of this book, you have been transformed from a cheerful, trusting soul with unflagging faith in the powers that be into a suspicious, angry skeptic and cynic who can't sit though a thirty-second news teaser without muttering and gesturing and foaming at the mouth. It's okay. You don't have to thank me. I'd do the same for anyone. Anyway, if I have truly done what I hoped to do in this book, I know you're not just wondering about Dan Rather's "sources," you're curious about mine, too. Who are these investigators and authorities I'm citing here? Are they really experts? Could they be delusional, paranoid wackos out to undermine everything we hold sacred? (Judging from what I see on TV, what we hold sacred is a sport utility vehicle the size of a Boeing 757 and non-yellowing floor wax.) Could they be—horror of horrors—CIA?

That's why I arranged an interview with the one and only Jim Marrs. Since the Kennedy assassination, Jim Marrs has proven himself to be the undisputed king of conspiracy and the potentate of righteous paranoia. His first book, *Cross-fire,* was a *New York Times* best-seller and a major source for Oliver Stone's film *JFK.* His latest work, *Alien Agenda,* has become a counterculture classic, offering proof upon proof that we are not alone in the universe . . . and I'm not talking about some weird molecule stuck in the middle of a Martian meteorite, either.

Are the conspiracy experts and researchers like Jim Marrs, who've literally risked their lives in the pursuit of truth, the real deal? Like I've said, don't go by me. In this section, I've gone straight to the source to bring you the most up-to-date information on some of the most important events and issues in alternative theory today, from the assassination of John Kennedy to the crash at Roswell, New Mexico, to the latest in alien abduction theory. The truth from Marrs. Read this next section. Then judge for yourself.

# 25

I'm Strictly a
She-Male G-Man

*I* wasn't going to write about J. Edgar Hoover in this book. He was such a slimy character that just typing his name made me feel as though I had been painted with sweat, then rolled in chiffon. But J. Edgar Hoover figured prominently in nearly every defining story of this century—including the election of JFK, the president's murder and probably its cover-up, and the government's inquiries into the existence of UFOs. Needless to say, Hoover has been a central character in Jim Marrs's research . . . and in my nightmare.

The proverbial lowlife who rose to the highest echelons of power, a man whose name has become synonymous with naked hypocrisy and the most outrageous abuse of power, John Edgar Hoover was an unlikely choice for America's top cop. A notorious thughugger, Hoover vacationed with top-level mobsters and pocketed payoffs from questionable colleagues such

*Yeah, and Having a Vagina Is Incidental to Being Female . . .* **Justice is incidental to law and order.**
—*FBI director J. Edgar Hoover*

## Conspiracy or Coincidence?
## Live by the Headache, Die by the Headache

J. Edgar Hoover was a person who gave a lot of people—including several presidents, attorneys general, alleged Communists, and certainly the designers of women's undergarments—a nagging pain. The question is, did someone give him in return Excedrin Headache number infinity?

Having endured nearly fifty years of Hoover's tyranny, by 1972 virtually every powerful person in every walk of life was ready to see the FBI director go—and it didn't really matter to them whether the miserable old fuck went horizontally or vertically. It was no secret that Richard Nixon (as did others before him) wanted nothing more than to force the FBI director to retire. But by then Hoover had amassed such a stockpile of dirt on his political enemies that he had made himself virtually fireproof. This, it is speculated, may have left his opponents no option. If Hoover wouldn't accept a retirement party, maybe he'd prefer a state funeral.

The scuttlebutt goes as follows: In the winter of 1972, Hoover became the target of two operations. The first was a break-in attempt during which "burglars" ("burglars" did a booming business in Washington in 1972) attempted to enter Hoover's house and steal documents that were thought to be potentially damaging to the president. Considering who the president was, that scenario is not far-fetched, but the attempt failed. Several weeks later, however, operatives did manage to break into Hoover's boudoir, where they planted a number of deadly poison tablets in Hoover's aspirin stash.

According to Anthony Summers, the author of *The Secret Life of J. Edgar Hoover,* the poison used was thiophosphate—a compound found in insecticides that is highly toxic to human beings. If it is ingested, thiophosphate can cause a sudden and fatal heart seizure. The body of J. Edgar Hoover was discovered near his bed on the morning of May 2, 1972, by Clyde Tolson.

But did the FBI director die of natural causes—or was he forced to take a job ouster lying down? We can't be sure. Thiophosphate can be detected in the body for only a few hours after death. To the best of my knowledge, no such testing was conducted. But Hoover's physician, Dr. Robert Choisser, was certainly caught off guard by his patient's demise. He is quoted in Summers's book as saying: "I was rather surprised by his sudden death, because he was in good health."

Funny . . . Jim Marrs cites seventy-seven JFK assassination witnesses whose next of kin might have said the same thing.

as Mafia bigwig Frank Costello while stubbornly insisting that organized crime didn't exist. ("Mafia? What Mafia? I don't see any Mafia.") His crime-fighting techniques included payoffs, bribes, buggings, seductions, druggings, and worse—with lit-

tle or no regard for the legalities of his activities. And he loved gambling, particularly at organized-crime-run horse tracks. In fact, he loved it nearly as much as he hated John and Robert Kennedy, the brothers who were working to put the Mafia out of business before, perhaps, the Mob did the same for them.

But what made J. Edgar Hoover what he was—that is, an evil, inflated bully—was not his rank or his title but the vast arsenal of confiden-

*I'm a Commie, You're a Commie, He's a Commie, She's a Commie, Wouldn't You Like to Be a Commie, Too?*
**The communist official will probably live in a modest neighborhood. His wife will attend the corner grocery store, his children attend the local school. If a shoe store or butcher shop is operated by a Party member, the official will probably get a discount on his purchases.**
—*J. Edgar Hoover,* Masters of Deceit: The Story of Communism and How to Fight It

## How You Can Screw Your Way to a Great Job as the President of the United States

J. Edgar Hoover was such a fascinating paradox, wasn't he? I mean, he blackmailed people his goons discovered were gay, yet he was carrying on a homosexual relationship himself. He knew that dark colors are more slenderizing and that it's crucial to maintain an elongating line, especially when you're a large man, yet he was partial to red flapper dresses. And, most of all, although he loathed and despised John Kennedy, he—Hoover—was responsible for getting him his gig as president. What . . . you didn't know that FBI Fun Fact? Well, neither did I until Jim Marrs clued me in.

Listen to this. In the early days of World War II, John Kennedy was a handsome young ensign-around-Washington. Kennedy was in Naval Intelligence then, which is a little-known fact. And I guess he was taking it pretty seriously that he was "in the service," because he was servicing a lot of women then, but mostly he was schtupping a former beauty queen from Denmark named Inga Arvad.

Now, when you're an incredibly good-looking man who's wearing a really spiffy uniform and whose father is as rich as God and you've got a cushy assignment in D.C. because Dad is also an ambassador to England, you don't have to do a lot of talking and explaining to women. You just show up and boom—that's foreplay. And when you're a really hot-looking beauty queen from Denmark, where everybody has mad, frantic sex for eight months a year, then they all jump off buildings because they are suffering from chronic light deprivation, you don't have to do much talking, either. So Inga Arvad never mentioned to JFK that she had actually met Adolf Hitler. And she never mentioned that J. Edgar Hoover believed she was a Nazi spy and that her apartment was bugged by the FBI.

Anyway, so there's dirty old man J. Edgar, listening in on the fun at Inga Arvad's apartment, and who does he pick up but Joe Kennedy's son! Of course, he went straight to the ambassador and told him everything, and when he did, Joe Kennedy decided that the best thing to do would be to get his son transferred out of Washington and into another nice desk job where the family jewels and Jack's reputation could be protected. But Jack had other ideas. If he was going to be transferred, he insisted, he would accept only a transfer into combat.

And the rest is history. JFK was put in command of PT-109, which was cut in half by a Japanese ship. Kennedy risked his life to rescue his crewmen and became a hero. That notoriety enabled him to win a seat in Congress. And his work in Congress paved his way to the White House, where he proved to be more irritating to J. Edgar Hoover than a gerbil suppository.

tial files he accumulated on the thousands of men and women he considered potential enemies. From debts to questionable business dealings to family scandals to the sexual peccadilloes of the rich and famous, Hoover sucked it all in—threatening to spit it all back out whenever an unfortunate victim balked at doing his bidding. That's why, throughout his forty-eight-year reign of terror, Hoover had so much real power that U.S. presidents routinely bypassed their own attorneys general to plead their cases directly to the head of the FBI.

But blackmail can be stamped "Return to Sender." It can end up right back where it came from, especially if the one collecting the secrets happens to be hiding a few of his own. And according to Hoover biographer Anthony Summers, Hoover's forays into buggery didn't always include listening devices. Although the FBI director tended to target homosexuals, it has been revealed that he carried on a long-term intimate relationship with his second-in-command at the bureau,

Clyde Tolson. And that's not all. Although Hoover was careful to walk the walk and talk the talk of a rough, tough G-man, he was also able to cut a rug in a pair of spiked pumps . . . or a really hot garter belt . . . or, as attorney Roy Cohn witnessed, in a red flapper-style dress with a black feather boa around his neck.

So what are you supposed to take away from all this? First, accessories are everything, aren't they? That dress wouldn't have been shit without the boa, and not even the whole Justice Department could convince me otherwise. Second, it's possible that the Mafia knew as much about Hoover as he knew about everyone else . . . and that they used this information to keep him from going after them. And third, if J. Edgar Hoover wasn't actively involved in the death of John Kennedy, he was almost certainly a passive participant. Can I prove it? Of course not. In the years since his death, a litany of evil deeds has been linked to this duplicitous, power-mad, government-sanctioned thug, including the Kent State shootings, the McCarthy hearings, and the formation of a secret Mafia/FBI hit squad. Though Hoover's complicity in these cases can't be proven, these actions could not have taken place without at least his knowledge.

As Hoover's case proves, knowledge is power. Especially if it's the kind of knowledge you can only get by ferreting through someone's garbage can.

# 26

# Anybody Up There?

It's hard for me to believe, but there are still plenty of people who remain unconvinced that intelligent life exists anywhere in the universe other than Earth. These people would undoubtedly be shocked to learn that I am unconvinced, sometimes for weeks on end, that there is intelligent life anywhere in the United States—particularly in Washington, D.C., or in any Department of Motor Vehicles from Boston to L.A.

## 1600—Life in the Margins

**The Dominican monk Giordano Bruno was burned at the stake for suggesting that other worlds besides the Earth may be inhabited. Here we are four centuries later, and those who dare suggest the same notion as Brother Bruno are now burned at the intellectual stake until their credibility is incinerated.**

Considering that a good part of the rest of this book deals with UFOs, extraterrestrials, and other space junk, it is best that we make our case for off-Earth life straightaway (Off-Earth

# Hey . . . Who Knew?

Who knew that UFOs and extraterrestrials were real? Well, Jim Marrs. Of course, nobody gets information like Jim Marrs. He attracts it . . . you know, the way the Kennedys attracted bullets. But according to Jim, the entire cast of the ongoing drama we call contemporary history knew UFOs and extraterrestrials were real . . . including John Kennedy himself.

A source connected to the military who has proven himself very credible recently provided Marrs with an interesting document. Dated November 12, 1963—less than a month before JFK was murdered—and signed by the ill-fated president, the document is directed to the head of the Central Intelligence Agency. It begins: "Subject Matter: Classification Review of All UFO Intelligence Files Affecting National Security." And in it JFK—as president and commander in chief—orders the CIA to gather up all their files on UFOs and turn them over to the White House.

Confused about the reason for Kennedy's cosmic consciousness? I was, too. But then Jim reminded me that, in 1963, Kennedy was already pursuing some joint space explorations with the Soviet Union. He was concerned that everyone involved might not be able to make a distinction between a true UFO and one of our own aircraft prototypes. If the Russians mistook a real UFO for one of our prototypes, it could have touched off World War III.

In fact, there is evidence that every president from Truman on knew about UFOs, so an accidental war caused by a case of mistaken identity was a big concern for several American presidents.

Anyway, it's all very fascinating. And if this document is correct, and Marrs has every reason to believe it is, we now have proof that Kennedy directed the CIA to collect all of their serious and classified UFO reports and turn them over to the Russians. And you can imagine how that would have sat with the coldest of the cold warriors. . . . Not only did Kennedy lose Cuba and Vietnam, now he wants to give them our space technology? Maybe we should kill that idea before it gets out of hand . . .

Life. Sounds like a magazine, doesn't it? It'd have articles like: "Radioactive Isotopes: They're Not Just for Breakfast Anymore!"). To do that, I went to three sources: science, history, and Jim Marrs.

Although anybody who has ever claimed to have seen men from Mars has been ridiculed and marginalized along with the assassination theorists and all the other kooks, most astronomers agree that the only member of our solar system other than Earth capable of supporting life is Mars. Although Mars isn't exactly up to its landing gear in oxygen and water, some scientists believe that there are beings on Mars and that they may have discovered ways to control or adapt to their environment. Some speculate that Martians live underground where the extremes in the planet's temperature would be moderated and the atmospheric pressure would be more conducive to life.

There are also scientists who do not pooh-pooh the idea of intelligent life existing on the planet Venus. And I'm not talking about Professor Irwin Corey, "The World's Foremost Authority," here, either. The mass and gravity of Venus are similar to those of Earth. Although the atmosphere of the planet is made up mostly of carbon dioxide and formaldehyde droplets, there is no reason to assume that other types of organisms couldn't live in an environment that would be strange to us. Hey . . . I live in France. Don't most Americans consider that country unconducive to life? Besides, with all that formaldehyde floating around, any civilization on Venus would certainly save on embalming costs. Beings go where the deals are.

Of course, for those of you who understand that there is a universe out there, these possibilities are only a drop in the bucket. (For the rest of you, here's a rundown: the universe is really big. It is even bigger than Wal-Mart. I'll leave you to ponder that vastness while I go on.) You know that our sun is a star with nine satellite planets. You also know that there are many other stars out there, all with satellite planets, many of which feature conditions that make habitation possible. The possibility for extraterrestrial life, then, is literally limitless.

By now you've probably decided whether you believe aliens exist or not. But if you haven't, it may help you to know that lots of other people—including people who spent many years on the state secret mailing list—believe it. And here are a few quotes to prove it.

> *The phenomenon [sic] reported is something real and not visionary or fictitious. . . . There are objects probably approximating the shape of a disc, of such appreciable size as to appear to be as large as a man-made aircraft. . . . The reported operating characteristics such as extreme rates of climb, maneuverability (particularly in roll), and action which must be considered evasive when sighted or contacted by friendly aircraft and radar lend belief to the possibility that some of the objects are controlled either manually, automatically or remotely.*
> —Gen. Nathan Twining, Chairman, Joint Chiefs of Staff, from a letter to the commanding general of the U.S. Army Air Forces, 1947

> *Unknown objects are operating under intelligent control. . . . It is imperative that we learn where UFOs come from and what their purpose is.*
> —Adm. Roscoe Hillenkoetter, first director of the CIA

> *I believe that these extraterrestrial vehicles and their crews are visiting this planet from other planets, which are obviously a little more technically advanced than we are here on Earth. I feel that we need to have a top-level, coordinated program to scientifically collect data from all over the Earth concerning any type of encounter and to determine how to interface with these visitors in a friendly fashion.*
> —American astronaut Gordon Cooper

# 27

## How Ten Myths About
## Aliens and UFOs
## Equal One Big Lie—
and Other Stuff That Just Doesn't Add Up

*A*dolf Hitler isn't known for his mathematical genius. I don't know why. Hitler was able to do what no mathematician before him could: he made $1 + 1 + 1 + 1 + 1 + 1 + 1 + 1 + 1 + 1 = 1$. And he did it by creating and using a psychological tactic that has become known as "the Big Lie."

The Big Lie is this: If you tell a lie that's big enough and you tell it often enough, people will believe you are telling the truth even when what you are saying is total crap.

Of course, just about everything Hitler ever said was a big lie. Yet some people believe that the use of the Big Lie died with Hitler in a bombproof bunker under the Berlin chancellery. (Actually, there is evidence that not even Adolf himself bit the big one in that bunker, but that's a conspiracy for another book.) The fact is the Big Lie is alive and well and used against us every day in every aspect of our lives. Best of all, it works—even if the "truths" that it's built on aren't particularly true! And if you don't believe me, check for it next time some politician decides to do something out of the ordinary, like bomb the shit out of some country the size of Rhode Island.

So, to recap: a whole bunch of little truths equals one big lie. Got that? Good. Because without that theorem and these little "truths," the government's story about the nonexistent UFOs just doesn't add up.

**1.** *We can't believe any evidence of UFOs because such evidence is purely anecdotal.* This premise hinges on the idea that we all agree that all people other than government officials and us are either nuts or full of shit. Of course, all you have to do is take a good look at the people around you in the 7-Eleven Slurpee line to realize there is a certain amount of truth to this observation. But if UFO sighting claimants and abductees are really the Forrest Gumps of the world, why do the powers that be go to such lengths to marginalize, neutralize, and silence them? Maybe life is just a box of chocolates . . . the real stuff is hidden in the middle of a bunch of overly sweetened fluff.

**2.** *Normal people like us don't know any wackos who believe they have seen UFOs.* My college geometry professor would call this a corollary to the previous entry. He'd still be calling it a corollary today if he hadn't been turned into quad-kill by the landing gear of a UFO.

Although this factoid might seem true, Jim Marrs believes we *all* know somebody who has seen, been in contact with, or has experienced some kind of extraterrestrial phenomenon. And to prove it, all you have to do is this: First, let it be known that you are interested in alien theory, then make it clear that you are open-minded enough to accept any anecdotal information you are offered without making any judgment.

Marrs predicts that if you just do those two things, people you have known all your life will suddenly come forward to tell their UFO story. Even if the people you know are conservative Republicans. (See Barry Goldwater's quote, page 156.)

**3.** *Terrifying tales about men from another planet . . . curiously similar UFO-related experiences . . . complaints of peculiar physical maladies and symptoms . . . these aren't the objective observations of independent witnesses. They are symptoms indicative of some kind of mass hysteria!* Oh, I see!

UFOs are too weird to be real, but a complex, heretofore undiagnosed, contagious, worldwide mass hysteria that people have been reporting for four thousand years . . . hey, we can buy that!

Too bad it's not true. As Jim Marrs told me: "Hey—if all we had were the abduction stories with no other evidence to back them up, no other UFO sightings, no history of UFO sightings, no ancient writings, I'd be the first to say it must be a mass psychosis. But the internal consistency of the contemporary abduction stories and everybody else's abduction stories, placed in the context of the last fifty years of UFOs, then placed in the larger context of man's prehistoric reports of people coming to Earth in flying machines . . . well, the evidence is just there."

So it is. And couldn't fifty years of dogged denial be considered a symptom of mass hysteria? Just wondering.

**4.** *If UFOs were real, they would make their existence known to our government.* Oh, absolutely! Any being—green, gray, or otherwise—with a story to tell is just dying to tell it to some bureaucrat. Hey, look how peacefully all those JFK assassination witnesses are resting after having gotten their stories off their chests!

**⊙FACTOID:**

**IT'S ALIEN TO US!**

There's a rumor that the designs for the Aurora, the Skyhawk, and the Stealth fighters are all based on alien technology. Jim Marrs told me, "There is no question that in the deserts of Nevada, particularly Groom Lake—which is also known as Area 51—we are testing some very, very futuristic and unusual craft and power plants. The only question is Where did we get this technology? According to Steven Greer of the Center for the Search for Extraterrestrial Intelligence, researchers now know of 165 former government and military employees who, if they knew they would not be prosecuted, would be willing to come forward right now and tell us just how we have come to engineer these UFOs."

But will scientists ever engineer a whistle-blower who can't be destroyed for telling the truth? Hey, babe . . . it's just a matter of time.

## Your Lips Are Saying "No, No, No," But Your Subconscious Is Saying "Yes, Yes, Yes!"

To be honest with you, I think the idea of a human happily undergoing medical procedures at the hands of a creature from another planet who is practicing proctology without a license is pretty weird. Then again, when I hear a seductive come-on like "Now I'm going to sample your genetic material," I can't help thinking, Oh, great . . . Nazis. As it turns out, that's probably just my personal quirk.

Many people who have agreed to go along with alien experimentation have told Jim Marrs that they don't regard the poking and probing as violation. To them, the experience was like a trip to a doctor. A doctor with grasshopperlike legs, antennae, an exoskeleton, and no piece of paper from Johns Hopkins, perhaps, but a doctor nonetheless.

How does Jim explain such cool? He says that many abductees have told him that they sense a metaphysical or spiritual "link" between them and their alien abductors. These people feel that, at some level, they have agreed to be abducted . . . and even diddled. Of course, a spiritual connection and a physical one are two different things. Sometimes when the abduction experience actually takes place in the three-dimensional world, it catches the human participants off guard and they are frightened or upset despite the consensual nature of the encounter. As Jim quipped to me, "Those little grays . . . they just don't have any bedside manner."

Every U.S. president since Truman has known perfectly well that we are being visited by booga-boogas from other worlds. In fact, Truman was so convinced of it, he instituted the National Security Council in part to protect us from any threats from the vast beyond.

But do aliens want to commune with our, ahem, leaders? Jim Marrs believes that they attempted to go that route and have since decided that Earth's bureaucrats aren't worth contacting.

As Marrs told me, "There's a good argument that can be made that, back in the forties and early fifties, extraterrestrials tried to make contact with certain leaders around the world. They were thinking, 'Okay—let's try and get the story out and get you humans up to speed with the rest of the intergalactic community.' But what they found was that these leaders, probably ours as well as those in the Eastern bloc and everywhere else, were afraid that acknowledging ETs would cause them to lose power. Plus, of course, each country wanted to keep the technology to themselves.

"So the ETs said, Well, this is a screwy situation, and over a period of time they decided to simply bypass the leadership and appeal to the common people, which is what led to the recent increase in sightings and abductions."

**5.** *There is no earthly reason for the government to withhold credible evidence that ETs exist.* If we aren't publicly acknowledging UFOs, it is because the evidence proving their existence isn't there. If the powers that be aren't acknowledging UFOs, it's because they fear for their jobs!

Check out this excerpt from an article that appeared in the *New York Times* on December 15, 1960:

MANKIND IS WARNED TO PREPARE FOR
DISCOVERY OF LIFE IN SPACE
*Brookings Institution Report Says
Earth's Civilization Might Topple if Faced
by a Race of Superior Beings*

Washington, Dec. 14 (UPI)—Discovery of life on other worlds could cause the Earth's civilization to collapse, a federal report said today.

This warning was contained in a research report given to the National Aeronautical and Space Administration with the recommendation that the world prepare itself mentally for the eventuality.

The report, prepared by the Brookings Institution,

said "while the discovery of intelligent life in other parts of the universe is not likely in the immediate future, it could nevertheless happen at any time." Discovery of intelligent beings on other planets could lead to an all-out effort by Earth to contact them, or it could lead to sweeping changes or even the downfall of civilization, the report said.

Even on Earth, it added, "societies sure of their own place have disintegrated when confronted by a superior society. . . ."

Can a society that debates whether ketchup constitutes a vegetable be called a "civilization"? I've got my doubts.

Beyond that, given the choice, with whom would you rather cast your lot? A career politician who, in twenty years, hasn't figured out how to provide health care for most of our citizens, or a being who knows the secrets of the universe, has mastered intergalactic travel, and may even be able to vaporize people who piss him off? There you go. Bear that in mind the next time you cast your vote for Trent Lott.

**6.** *There is something vaguely blasphemous about belief in aliens. That's why God Him-/Herself is anti-alien.* Hear me: Most people who believe in God or a higher power or whatever believe that his or her God is the God of everyone in the universe. So what's the problem if (S)He is also the God of little gray men who drive around in spaceships rather than Hondas? If one God can be the God of Attila the Hun and Mother Teresa, (S)He can be the God of everybody.

Of course, there are people who believe that single-parent families, dancing while vertical, and PVC piping could also undermine all they hold sacred. But since what they hold sacred is a repressive status quo, I can only hope they're right.

So there. And don't make me go through this basic stuff again.

**7.** *Since UFOs could only have been created by a technologically superior civilization and no intelligent life exists in space, there can't be any UFOs at all.*

The airbags in our cars can be fatal. And you can't nuke a veggie burger that isn't frozen in the middle and burnt on the edges, sort of like your testicles if you've been standing too close. Considering the technological botch-jobs we live with every day, it is easy to believe that UFOs are so complex they could only have been created by some superior species. But according to what researchers have learned, that is simply not true.

Flying disks of human making were developed by the Nazis during World War II (see page 167). In fact, Werner von Braun and John Kennedy reportedly met a few times to discuss how the "spaceships" American scientists were developing might be fueled. (Hmm . . . and the next thing you know, Tang powdered drink mix hits the market. Is there a connection?)

But what makes this issue confusing to a lot of people is the fact that the "experts" are always trying to make UFOs an either/or situation. Either flying disks are created by human technology or they're something from outer space. And the truth is they're both.

What Jim Marrs told me is this: "There's no question that when we overran Germany at the end of World War II there were plans on the drawing board for flying disks: some powered by jet engines, but some powered by electromagnetism and other nonconventional power sources. The only question is, did the Nazis get to the point where they actually developed something that flew? That's where the controversy is."

In his book *Alien Agenda* Marrs tells a fascinating story about Werner von Braun and the SS officer Ernst Kammler.

## FACTOID:

### WHAT GOES UP DOES COME DOWN

Although there have been claims that people have been abducted by UFOs and returned mutilated or not returned at all, Jim Marrs knows of no documented reports of true intergalactic kidnapping. Therefore, putting Linda Tripp on the top of the Capitol Building with a sign that reads "Take Me, Little Gray Man" cannot be considered a solution.

Ernst Kammler was a high-ranking official who reported directly to Heinrich Himmler. He was also prominent within the Waffen-SS, so prominent, in fact, that at the end of the war, when the SS was pretty much taking over everything, he was put in charge of spiriting the Nazis' top-secret rocket programs (with scientists and V-2s, and all) to a safe haven near Munich in Bavaria. He told the scientists at that time that his plan was to give himself up to the Americans and to offer them the rocket scientists and the rockets—in other words, Germany's technology—in exchange for his life.

Sure enough, Kammler disappeared shortly thereafter—and was never heard of since. Of course, as we now know and as history records, when the Allies piled into Bavaria they captured Werner von Braun and the V-2 rockets and all that technology. So that makes me wonder: What technology did Kammler know about that allowed him to bond with the Allies? What plans did he take off with? And where did he get those plans? Were they pulled from German ingenuity or from a wrecked alien craft?

Which brings us to Number 8. . . .

**8.** *No American functionary has ever captured anything remotely resembling an alien spacecraft.*

Have we found wreckage? Shit, we're flying it! Jim Marrs told me about a case in Texas in the mid-eighties in which two women and a boy encountered what appeared to be a big glowing UFO surrounded by helicopters. The disk, they said, was airborne, but it was wobbling and spinning and flashing as though it were in some distress. You know, kind of like a 1972 Gremlin did before you put it up on blocks in your front yard.

Anyway, a few days later these people started experiencing some strange physical symptoms. Their skin was burned, their hair was falling out, and horrific lesions were developing on their bodies. They went to the doctor and were immediately diagnosed with radiation sickness.

Naturally, they pleaded their case with the United States government, saying, Hey—this was some kind of test you were doing and it harmed us and now we want some kind of compensation. But the government denied having any such technology, so the court threw it out.

Through sources Jim Marrs has developed in the military, he has learned that, in that particular case, they were testing a UFO—that is, an off-Earth craft—the military had captured or somehow acquired. To try and get it to go, they put a little nuclear power plant into it, like from a nuclear submarine. They believed they were going to fly it with this fission-based power plant in it. There they were, spewing radiation all over the place. Not that they're averse to exposing innocent citi-

---

### Be Afraid . . . Be Very Afraid. . . .

While the politicians live in fear that ET will touch down on the D.C. mall and leave skid marks all over their nice clean power base, and the religious leaders quake in their neckwear, wondering whether the faithful won't confuse a short, telepathic, pallid stranger (sounds like Kreskin, doesn't it?) for the One and Only Deity, here's something the rest of us can worry about!

Jim Marrs knows for sure that there are contingency plans in the government files right now for the day we have a major, undeniable, Phoenix-type UFO sighting. (You know what I'm talking about here . . . I'm talking about the day the mothership lands in the Safeway parking lot and blows Sam Donaldson's toupee off on the evening news.) According to Marrs's sources, the instant extraterrestrial visitors make themselves irrevocably known, that's when the government is going to step in and tell us all, "Okay—UFOs are real. Now you must give up every last shred of your civil and human rights so we can protect you."

It's a double-whammy deal: we concede the truth, but—oh, too bad—life as you know it is over. Still, it's better than the deal they offered Dorothy Kilgallen, *n'est-ce pas?*

zens to a little radiation now and then. Heck . . . who isn't looking forward to the day when strippers have three breasts?

**9.** *UFO "abductees" aren't troubled because they've been exposed to aliens. They are simply troubled people. Period.* Or are they? Jim Marrs suggests that the abductions we tend to hear about in the media are those that make for an exciting broadcast—i.e., precisely those that *are* traumatic, frightening, and/or painful. But that doesn't mean all abductees believe their encounters with aliens are akin to interstellar "date rape."

When we hear about alien abductions in books or on TV talk shows, we are generally hearing from those abductees who are seeking help or information or "communion" or guidance, and that's fine. There are plenty of people out there who can empathize with their experiences. But what we rarely hear about are the many, many people who have had alien encounters but did not regard them as painful or fearful. These people aren't looking for help or compassion or anything else. You don't hear about them because they don't need their experiences clarified by a talk-show host. Nor are they seeking the ridicule that goes hand in hand with going public.

As for the game of Name That Nut the "authorities" have been playing for the past half-century, isn't it possible that people who deny every possibility without ever looking at the evidence are the real nuts here? I mean, it's like blaming, say, the next schmo to walk past the Coke machine for a presidential assassination without any eyewitness testimony or proof! How sane is that?

**10.** *Free and democratic America is the most open and honest country in the world. No rational person believes there has been anything but a totally up-front and candid exchange of ideas on this and every other controversial subject.* Maybe public flogging isn't the preferred form of discipline in this country (but it *can* be if you're willing to pay for it!), but "free and democratic America" is no place to initiate an open and honest dialog about anything. Oliver Stone's film masterpiece *JFK* was lambasted by the critics before it was ever shown . . . and the intimidators have similarly trounced his latest work, an exposé of the controversial downing of Pan Am Flight 800. And that's only the beginning. The lifework of credible but politically incorrect researchers has gone unread. And people whose thoughts wander beyond the parameters of "acceptable" theory are routinely silenced, either professionally, politically, or, when necessary, physically. Open and honest? Tell that to Lee Harvey Oswald's corpse.

And the pervasive atmosphere of mistrust, intimidation, and fear has trickled down to the personal level. A friend of Jim Marrs's told him a story that illustrates this perfectly. It seems that when this friend was a college student, he and a buddy were driving along a highway at night when they saw a strange light. The light was not stationary, like a star . . . nor did it move in straight lines, like an airplane. It hovered, it dipped . . . it did things no conventional aircraft could possibly do. The men continued watching, in silence, until finally the craft just shot straight up in the sky and disappeared. At that, Marrs's friend turned to his companion in awe and remarked, "Wow! did you see that?" But instead of discussing what they had just witnessed, his friend just flew off the handle. He got very angry and snapped that he hadn't seen anything and just shut up about it.

For this man, if he didn't admit to seeing a UFO, he wouldn't have to deal with the truth of having seen a UFO. Unfortunately, this is the same attitude alternative historians and UFO researchers have been up against for fifty years, at the highest levels as well as at the most intimate. There are people in "open, honest America" who have seen and experienced these things firsthand but, in order to protect their reputations, careers, and relationships, will tell you that it didn't happen. Gather up a few hundred of those people and you've got an informational stonewall. Convince several thousand men and women they'd rather not be this year's Oliver Stone and you've effectively blacked out the truth.

Now, what were you saying about those strange lights you saw? Nothing? Yeah, that I what I thought.

Do *you* see a problem? I'll bet you don't. Do you see a big difference between getting your information from independent researchers, like Jim Marrs, and getting fed the same old lies by national media? I'll bet you do. For one thing, researchers are willing to address the issues. *Any* issues. They don't pretend evidence isn't there when it is, or that it is there when it isn't. They don't have to lie to protect the guilty, because they aren't getting paid by the guilty. And their information isn't filled with disclaimers, innuendo, or attempts to mislead or distort. Eliminating redundancies like those leaves a lot of room on a page for truth.

Of course, if you prefer your information watered down, twisted, or politically sanitized, you can still get your news from the fifth network, CIA. But to those of you who don't, I say, stay tuned. The truth is in here.

# UFOs

# 28

## What the Hell Fell?

*What if all of us in the world discovered that*
*we were threatened by an outer . . .*
*a power from outer space, from another planet?*
—RONALD REAGAN

*Y*eah, *what if?*

The quote above is real. Which is to say that Ronald Reagan really said it. And I'm not surprised. Ronald Reagan was a throwback to the 1940s and '50s and during those decades UFOs were a big rage. In fact, the term "flying saucer" came into existence in 1947 when an airplane pilot named Kenneth Arnold reported that he had played "catch me, catch me" with nine strange aircraft in the skies over the American Northwest. Since the sighting took place in broad daylight, Arnold was able to clearly describe the boomerang-shaped crafts he saw. He was also able to describe their curious movements. The UFOs, he said, moved the way a saucer would if it were skipping across the surface of a lake. Some reporter distilled Arnold's description into the phrase "flying saucer," and we've been using it ever since.

Needless to say, reporters in the forties and fifties made it their business to interview every schmo that claimed he had had an "encounter." But other than Arnold, it always seemed as though they were interviewing the same guy, the same farmer from somewhere like Devil's Asshole, Alabama. And the coverage would always start off the same way, with the reporter sticking one of those big round microphones in the farmer's face and asking him, Tell me, sir, what did you see? The story would always go something like this:

FARMER: *Well, let me get a grip on the situation here. Tell you where I was. I'll tell you what I saw. Let's see . . . oh! I remember where I was now. I was, uh . . . I was, uh . . . I was settin' up on my front porch, see? And my twin albino boys, they was, uh . . . they wuz carvin' their names in each other's feet, you know what I mean? And my wife was inside, trying to find herself in a mirror, okay? That's my Martha. Can knock a boil off a weevil's testicle with a wad of chaw from forty paces, but I never said she was a bright woman.*

REPORTER: (excited now) *Okay. Then what?*

FARMER: *Anyway, you see where my dog's takin' a shit by that barn over there? Look—there he goes now. Go, Spot, go! Anyway, this cigar-shaped object come down outa the sky. And this little bug-eyed green sumbitch got out, looked around, and ate one of my hogs. Then he ate my wife. Well, she didn't seem to mind that too much. Matter of fact, she went with him.*

(Shouts to the sky) *Martha, if you can hear me, I've got a sink full of dishes here. I've got two bloody-footed boys. You'd better get back down here. And don't gimme no shit about what dimension you're in.*

I know what you're thinking. You're thinking, What would a farmer know about different dimensions? What would a farmer know about UFOs? Hey, if Barry Goldwater could be convinced that aliens exist (see sidebar on page 156), someone as open-minded as a farmer can know a lot. Aliens visit us all the time. UFOs *land* and leave bizarre things behind. I mean, where else could all those minivans have come from?

Anyway, the point is this: farmers and pilots and regular

## Coincidence or Conspiracy?
## Don't Any Normal People See Aliens?

If you read the tabloids you may believe that it is actually necessary to have albino twin boys, webbed feet, or some other outward sign of inbreeding to encounter aliens. This is false. A lot of pilots have encountered aliens, and they're not even allowed to have long hair, let alone third nipples.

Besides, researchers suggest that government sources have actually planted less-credible and even downright weird claimants in order to bolster the belief that all witnesses are delusional, attention junkies, or nuts of another sort.

people are great UFO witnesses because they aren't afraid to tell people exactly what they have seen. Unlike the government and the National Aeronautic and Space Administration (NASA). Why, they wouldn't admit the possibility that aliens walk among us even if someone at the very highest levels of government was discovered to have abducted young women, probed their genitalia with strange cigar-shaped objects, and marked their clothing with viscous fluids impervious to virtually any cleaning system on Earth. Okay, so maybe that's a bad example. But what has become known as the Roswell Incident is a case in point.

On July, 2, 1947, just a few days after Kenneth Arnold's UFO encounter, rancher Mac Brazel happened upon some peculiar wreckage on his spread near

 **FACTOID:**

**THE SHAPE OF THINGS TO COME**
Researchers have identified three basic UFO shapes: the flying disk or "saucer," the cigar-shaped craft, and the boomerang-shaped UFO. If the suspicious-looking entity hovering over your home is irregularly shaped, don't panic: it isn't a spacecraft. It's probably just a radioactive cloud released into the atmosphere by your own government.

Corona, New Mexico. The wreckage was strewn over about a half mile of Brazel's property and defied identification. From the debris, the rancher collected a few samples, including a piece of an odd tinfoil-like material that was easily molded, folded, and creased, but popped immediately back into its original shape the moment it was released, and a dowel fabricated of what appeared to be light plastic that, unlike plastic, could not be scratched, burned, or melted. Over the next few days, he showed it to a number of friends and family members who were quite interested in the find, though the civilians were hardly as agitated by the discovery as were officials from the nearby Roswell Army Air Field.

Major Jesse Marcel was immediately dispatched to inspect Brazel's evidence. That same day, he filled two Army vehicles with as much wreckage as he and a colleague could collect and sent it to Washington for analysis. The following day he returned to the ranch, where more debris— including a metal assemblage that measured some four feet in length—was gathered. Some of

## DON'T BARRY THE EVIDENCE!

In his lifetime, Barry Goldwater was called a lot of things—sometimes by me—but one thing the conservative former senator from Arizona was *never* called is a wild-eyed conspiracy nut. So it's important to note that even he became frustrated with government stonewalling on the issue of UFO research. He wrote this letter on the twenty-eighth of March, 1975, to a group of UFOlogists: "The subject of UFOs is one that has interested me for some long time. About ten to twelve years ago I made an effort to find out what was in the building at Wright-Patterson Air Force Base where the information is stored that has been collected by the Air Force, and I was understandably denied the request. It is still classified above Top Secret. I have, however, heard that there is a plan under way to release some, if not all, of this material in the near future. I'm just as anxious to see this material as you are, and I hope we will not have to wait much longer."

Barry Goldwater died on May 29, 1998. And before the material hidden at Wright-Patterson is released, I probably will, too.

## Marrs on Roswell

As Jim Marrs told me in an exclusive interview for this book, he has been in contact with two men who, over time, have proven themselves to be very credible UFO researchers. One has held a very important position in defense work, and both have very good track records for veracity. Anyway, these contacts recently provided Marrs with a document anyone curious about Roswell would find edifying.

The document is a copy of a classified report dated July 22, 1947. From the marks and initials scrawled on it, it is apparent to Marrs that this document had been widely circulated—including among the Joint Chiefs of Staff. The document acknowledges that two crash sites were located by government investigators, one at a ranch near Corona approximately seventy-five miles northwest of the town of Roswell and another approximately twenty miles southeast of the town of Socorro. According to the memorandum, the wreckage at the Socorro site was stirring up some excitement. That's because, according to the document, "the wreckage at this site contained the majority of structural detail of the craft's airframe, propulsion and navigation technology."

But wait—there's more! The document goes on to say that "the recovery of five bodies in a damaged escape cylinder precluded investigation."

Five bodies in an escape cylinder? Sounds authentic, doesn't it? Well, hold on to your pressure helmet. The document also suggests that the personnel who assessed the wreckage also determined that the wreckage was not of the type "belonging to any aircraft, rocket, weapons or balloon tests that are currently conducted from surrounding bases."

So the weather-balloon story was full of hot air . . . and we were the last to know! Surprise!

the "space junk" was transported to Wright-Patterson Air Force Base in Dayton, Ohio, while other samples were sent back to Roswell.

The military being what it is—a tight-assed, tight-lipped government organ and armed agent of paranoia—word filtered down through all of the personnel associated with the cleanup that this was a top-secret investigation. But the dictum came too late. News that the government had acquired the remains of a crashed "flying disk" had already been released by Wright-Patterson's public

## THERE'S A METHOD TO THIS MADNESS.

Unless a UFO decides to splatter itself all over the north forty, a farmer's life is quite simple. His encounters—usually with barnyard animals—are easy to classify. He meets up with, say, a chicken, and what happens next is either legal or illegal. End of story. Save the details for the judge.

Not so for encounters with aliens. The Hynek Classification System (devised by—surprise!—Dr. J. Allen Hynek) was designed to categorize UFO sightings and human–alien encounters so researchers could more easily track manifestations by type and location. The designations are as follows.

- *Nocturnal Light:* Any strange light or lights (i.e., not generated by aircraft, meteors, etc.) visible in the sky.
- *Daylight Disk:* Unidentified flying objects of any shape (see descriptions on page 155) visible in the sky during daylight hours.
- *Radar-Visuals:* UFOs located by radar and verified visually by eyewitnesses.
- *Close Encounter of the First Kind:* A UFO that hovers or passes within five hundred feet of an eyewitness.
- *Close Encounter of the Second Kind:* A UFO that leaves physical evidence of its presence, including burns on trees or the ground, radio and television interference, paralysis to humans, etc.
- *Close Encounter of the Third Kind:* A UFO in which an occupant or occupants are clearly visible to eyewitnesses.
- *Close Encounter of the Fourth Kind:* A human is abducted by aliens.
- *Close Encounter of the Fifth Kind:* Alien–human communication.

information office. Moreover, the story was being circulated by Teletype and broadcast by several New Mexico radio stations. But as an Albuquerque station was broadcasting its coverage of the UFO crash, its transmission was suddenly interrupted by a Teletyped message from the FBI. It read: "Attention Albuquerque: Cease transmission. Repeat: Cease transmission. National security item."

The next day, the Air Force released a clarification, stating unequivocally that the mysterious debris that had been recovered from Mac Brazel's ranch had turned out to be nothing more than the remains of a weather balloon. A believable conclusion? Hardly. The authorities placed Brazel under house arrest for more than a week and warned him never to speak of what he had found. That seems a little extreme, considering the man supposedly found a benign meteorological device. What would they have done if he had happened upon a barometer? Put his eyes out?

So what the hell fell in Roswell? Many conspiracy theorists believe the original story promulgated by the military: that a spacecraft from another planet crashed near that small city. They also believe that the evidence seized by the Army Air Corps includes the ship and the bodies of its inhabitants and that both are currently being housed in a mysterious building known as Hangar 18 on Wright-Patterson Air Force Base. Others accept the theory that an experimental craft of American make crashed in Roswell. Whatever theory you subscribe to, the bottom line is this: the government has taken great pains to make sure that we'll never know.

# 29

## Hallelujah,
## It's Raining Spacemen!

You know, I love cops. Of course, I love them more now that I play one on TV. I go through a red light, I run over a pedestrian, cop pulls me over, takes one look at me, smiles, and says, "Oh. It's you." I literally can't get arrested anymore. But there's a big difference between West Coast cops and the police in the East. West Coast cops are obsessed with traffic. New York cops don't give a shit about traffic. You can be driving along the streets of Manhattan sixty miles an hour with a beer between your legs, seat belt flapping out the door, a big joint in your mouth, go through five red lights, pass a New York cop, and he'll yell, "Yo! Bring me a cup of coffee on your way back, okay?"

So what's this got to do with aliens? Just this: judging from the number of UFO crashes that have

*I can assure you the flying saucers, given that they exist, are not constructed by any power on Earth.*
*—President Harry Truman, 1950*

been reported over the years, it seems to me that our alien brothers could use some traffic direction.

You think your insurance company is giving you a hard time? Check out these accident reports:

## SHE'S BA-ACK . . .

In May 1947, an American journalist reported that a mysterious flying ship had crashed in Spitzbergen, Norway, and that British scientists and airmen were quietly investigating the wreckage. That journalist was . . . you guessed it! Dorothy Kilgallen! Although the story was only a passing blip for one day in the U.S. media, the Swedish military acknowledged the craft's otherworldly origin before the item was silenced by the military.

*December 22, 1909:* A story that made front-page headlines from New York to the Midwest detailed the crash of a large spacecraft in an area west of Chicago. Although the crash was reportedly witnessed by thousands, the wreckage was never found.

*May 1947:* A strange airship splatters itself across the scenery of Spitzbergen, Norway. And the airship wasn't all that was strange about this case. (See boxed text at left.)

*July 2, 1947:* On this date a flying saucer abruptly stopped flying over Roswell, New Mexico. The wreck and the subsequent shoddy cover-up is believed to have

## Abra-Cadaver

After reading about all those very terrestrial mishaps (the crashes listed above are just the tip of the iceberg) you may have the impression that planet Earth is littered with more quivering masses of unidentifiable greenish-grayish goo than you'd find on the buffet table at a Hadassah lunch. And, according to many researchers, you'd be right. UFOlogists believe that scientists have confiscated the remains of at least 115 aliens who bit the dust on the Blue Planet—and that another eleven aliens were purportedly taken alive.

launched a million government skeptics, countless researchers, and innumerable theorists, some of whom believe that at least one survivor and the bodies of several other extraterrestrials were recovered from the crash.

*February 13, 1948:* When three radar units tracked a nose-diving aircraft northeast of Aztec, New Mexico, Secretary of State George Marshall asked that a party of investigators search the area. They discovered a demolished thirty-foot disk and, some believe, the remains of a dozen charred humanoids.

*April 1950:* Mr. E. C. Bossa discovers saucer wreckage and the bodies of four aliens in a remote area of Argentina. When he returned to the site with a friend the next day, the saucer was gone—but both men glimpsed a cigar-shaped UFO in the skies above them.

## No Shit!

I know what you're thinking. You're thinking, Richard—I see things splattered on the road all the time. How can I tell if what I'm looking at is an ET or just a really strange-looking possum? *The UFO Crash/Retrieval Syndrome* by Leonard H. Stringfield should help you make sense of the carnage. As a rule of thumb: ETs don't have thumbs, though many have one finger that is noticeably longer than the others. These fingers might come in handy when scratching certain hard-to-reach places, but reportedly, ETs don't have those places, either. According to doctors who claim to have taken part in numerous alien autopsies, aliens have no digestive system, no intestines, no alimentary canal, and no rectal area.

In addition, ETs have small noses and mouths, gray or ashen reptile-like skin, and large heads in which they store brains that measure about 500 cc larger than those of average humans. (They sound just like Calvin Klein models, don't they?)

*May 21, 1953:* An Air Force helicopter pilot reports that he was summoned to the scene of a UFO crash in Kingman, Arizona. The pilot, who had been recruited to help in the recovery of the craft, claimed to have seen a large, metal disk that had impacted the ground so hard it plowed up a furrow of earth some twenty inches deep. In an affidavit published in *UFO* magazine, he also claimed that a space-suited alien was found in the wreckage, dead.

*November 9, 1974:* A group of teenagers report having seen a glowing craft crash into a lake outside of Carbondale, New Jersey. The boys were detained by the police while a disk-shaped craft was recovered from the water. Several days later, local authorities reported that a railroad lantern and battery were the only things found submerged in the water and that the teenagers' story had been a hoax. (Refresh my memory: there was no Mauser in the Book Depository, right? And there was only one Oswald. Right.)

*May 6, 1978:* A massive, glowing UFO crashed into a 13,000-foot mountain in Padcaya, Bolivia. A search party made up of military personnel and scientists was sent to investigate but found nothing.

# 30

## Out There or
## Down Here?
### Where Oh Where Do They Come From?

Where do aliens come from? Some people think that all known alien life-forms can be traced to an Airstream trailer found abandoned in the South Bronx in 1952 with a sticker on it that read "If This Thing's Rockin', Don't Come Knockin'," but I don't believe it. And neither do researchers. But even conspiracy theorists don't agree on where aliens come from or why they have made their presence known.

> **I was looking at them as extraterrestrials.**
> —Soviet astrophysicist Roald Sagadeyev after meeting with U.S. scientists

Most people who believe in UFOs accept that unexplained spacecraft are just that: complex transport systems created by technologically superior beings from outer space or realms beyond our reach. But others believe that UFOs come from a place much closer to home—and, perhaps, with a much darker purpose.

Is it possible that UFOs could be of human making? There is evidence to support that idea—and its history takes shape

# ADOLF, HERMANN, AND ME

Some years ago I found out that the day I was born, August 4, 1944, was the day Anne Frank was arrested. I know I cannot logically take responsibility for what happened to either of us . . . my arrival, her arrest . . . my birth, her death . . . but discovering this common thread between Anne Frank and me has set me off on a journey of personal and historical epiphany. In fact, our lives seem so deeply and inextricably connected that I can't help but feel that Anne Frank's capture and my intellectual freedom are somehow karmically related.

Shortly after discovering the coincidence surrounding my birthdate (are there any coincidences, really?), I began examining the whole Nazi thing—both as a Jew and as a person who came of age during a time marked by a mysterious presidential assassination. With more than six hundred titles available on the events in Dealey Plaza and potentially thousands on German history, I knew it would take me years to uncover everything that had been hidden from me. Then it happened! I discovered with perverse awe that there was a connection between my two obsessions. There are researchers who believe that former Nazis who, by the 1960s, had become part of the booming military-industrial complex were among the billionaires who were opposed to ending the Cold War and therefore conspired to have Kennedy killed.

Can you imagine? Probably not! You seem sane enough. Anyway, just having this information made me angry and delirious at the same time. OK, I admit it. There is something incredibly seductive about knowing something that is not known to the general public. But even that sublime feeling is nothing compared to the satisfaction that comes with knowing you have asked the questions that matter to you most—and have come up with an answer that addresses the historical significance as well as the deepest personal aspects of your lifelong driving obsession.

during World War II, in the secret factories where the Nazis developed what they hoped would be their "wonder weapons."

In 1945, German scientists had already been experimenting with flying-disk theory for many years. So when it seemed that World War II might take a nasty turn, Adolf Hitler began planning a last-ditch scenario in which he would dazzle the Allies with the "Wunderwaffen" his scientists had devised, including working flying saucers. Although the Germans couldn't get their "spacecraft" off the ground in time to win the war, their advances did save them. American intelligence was so intrigued by what the Nazi scientists had discovered about saucer design and propulsion that a secret deal between the United States and Nazi Germany was struck. Immediately after the war, a think tank of over four hundred top Nazi scientists in the field of saucer research and development and up to fifteen thousand scientific and technical personnel were quietly folded into the American aerospace industry in an action known as "Operation Paperclip." Since then, researchers believe, the United States has been filling secret hangars with prototypes—and the skies with functioning saucers. And they're not the only ones who think so. A 1950 article titled "Flying Saucers: The Real Story" published in *U.S. News & World Report* declared that the "U.S. Built [the] First One in 1942." Timothy Good's book *Above Top Secret* also made this claim.

So what about the hundreds of claimants who believe they have seen, communicated with, or been abducted by little grayish men with very high foreheads and very large probes? Those who subscribe to this particular theory also believe that these people are either secret government agents who hope to steer public attention away from evidence of real home-made saucers or innocent dupes. There is also a contingent who believe that certain Hollywood producers and writers have been recruited by the government to provide the world's movie buffs with an indelible—and phony—image of space-men and their crafts to further obscure the possibility of U.S. involvement in flying saucer technology.

## Conspiracy or Coincidence?
## German Engineering Takes Off

Immediately following World War II, high-ranking British officials announced that they were working on some extremely revolutionary new aircraft—crafts that could fly thousands of miles an hour using some very unconventional power plants. Could the British have been picking the brains of Nazi war criminals and scientists working on top-secret rocketry? Let me put it this way. The U.K. had been crippled by the war. When your country's capital has been reduced to rubble, technology isn't usually your first concern. Nor were the British known for sophisticated rocketry. So draw your own conclusions.

In an interesting twist, Marrs also believes it is possible that the impoverished British may have teamed up with the Canadians to develop this technology. Shortly after the British announcement, it was revealed that a disk-shaped craft was being designed and tested in western Canada. In June of 1947, Kenneth Arnold reported his encounter with a number of flying disks in the airspace near Mount Rainier! What are we talking about here? We're talking about an area right across the border from where they're supposedly working on this flying disk! We're also talking about some real evidence that the intelligence agencies and the militaries of several foreign countries were trying to develop their own flying saucers in the 1940s—and they couldn't have done it without a little help from their enemies.

By now you're probably wondering what the motivation might be for all of this duplicity and mass manipulation. Here are a few options from among which you can choose. Some UFO researchers, like John Keel, believe that the UFOs are meant to infiltrate society like a "Trojan Horse," then manipulate us to further some as yet undisclosed government agenda.

What kind of an agenda? Well, if a flying saucer landed in your yard and broadcast a message saying that you should report immediately to a certain location or take up arms against some postcard country like Liechtenstein, or some benign group of people—say, for instance, the Little Sisters of Perpetual Misery—what would you do? Okay. That's just what Keel is getting at here.

Other theorists look back at the history of human civilization for clues. The sacred texts of nearly every known religion refer to visitations by strange beings who come from above to instruct and enlighten. Although these beings represent many diverse cultures, their magical manifestations always have the same psychological effect. Whether they're perceived as angels or messiahs or aliens or omens, visitors from "above" galvanize the beliefs, change the behavior, and motivate the actions of those who believe they have seen them. Could our government find a use for a large crowd of slack-jawed, unquestioning idolators? I'm not sure. Why don't you ask Adolf Hitler?

# 31

# What Do
# Extraterrestrials Want?

*P*eople say that flying saucers visit the Earth in order to be noticed. I don't believe it. I always thought that if flying saucers wanted to be noticed they wouldn't land in places like Devil's Asshole, Alabama. They'd land somewhere conspicuous, like on the White House lawn. Then they'd get coverage. Everybody would be watching.

You know how it would go. A ship would land in a cloud of smoky, foggy stuff. A hatch would open. And this creature, like a hundred thousand years ahead of us, would come floating out. Then, without ever moving his mouth or saying a word, he would communicate his message to us all:

ALIEN: *People of Earth. We have been in existence for billions and billions of years. We have traveled to the far reaches of the universes. And we've learned the three most important things of all. We will tell you these things once, and once only. Then we will leave your tiny planet.*
*Number one—brush after every meal.*

*Number two—don't go swimming until one hour after you eat.*

*Number three—cut off your balls and meet me behind the comet.*

You know, what is that all about? Cut off your balls? Cut off your *balls?* Put five dollars, a roll of quarters, and some Chap Stick in your pocket, then stop breathing so you'll go to a higher level? Excuse me, but did you ever hear of an elevator? Aliens from Alpha Centauri have heard of an elevator. You think they want you to cut off your balls? Aliens are into balls! They're forever probing someone's balls, taking specimens from someone's balls, tweezing hairs off someone's balls . . . they're like an intergalactic special prosecutor's office! So keep your balls, for Christ's sake. Get on an elevator. And stay away from cults like Hale-Bopp. Hale-Bopp isn't a path to enlightenment. It's a jazz expression from the forties. Hale Bopp. Ba-ba-do-ba-dee-ya, da-boo-da-dee. You know what I'm saying.

Okay—so if aliens didn't travel light-years to tell us to cut off our balls, what *do* they want? Here are a couple of theories. They may be disturbing, but they won't prevent you from dressing to the left.

*I Ain't Gonna Work on ET's Farm No More.* Some theorists believe that the Earth is actually an alien race's experimental farm. On this farm, humans are hybridized, that is, crossbred with aliens, to produce a race of men and women with enhanced telepathic or intellectual abilities. These superhumans can be—and many people believe are currently—used to fulfill any number of alien causes.

Certainly there is no lack of firsthand testimony on this theory. Books and periodicals and Web sites for abduction sur-

**FACTOID:**

**AND YOU THINK YOUR LAST BLIND DATE WAS WEIRD. . . .**

Gordon Creighton, the editor of the longest-running UFO magazine, *Flying Saucer Review,* believes that a significant percentage of the people you meet are actually half-alien, half-human—and some are 100 percent ET.

## HAVE YOU BEEN ABDUCTED?

The abduction of humans by aliens is traceable to the inception of written history. Needless to say, with epochs of evidence to draw upon, psychiatrists and other researchers have been able to identify a very distinct set of circumstances and symptoms common to true abduction cases. These signs include:

• *A feeling of paralysis or helplessness.* The abductee is transfixed by a very bright light or a humming sound. Shortly thereafter, he or she is transported by a strange energy. This movement occurs regardless of the abductee's will and puts the person in direct contact with one or more aliens.

• *Physical trauma.* The abductee becomes aware of strange, humanoid beings busily at work around him and may even describe large computerlike machines nearby. At some point, one of his captors begins a series of medical-type procedures, which may include the probing of body cavities, a type of brain surgery, or the forced extraction of sperm or ova. These procedures can be quite painful and traumatic.

• *Vivid memories.* The events of a real abduction can usually be recalled by the abductee without hypnosis or drug therapy or even a conscious effort to relax and remember. They may even cause post-traumatic stress disorder in some people.

• *A feeling that time has been lost.* Abductees—and even those people who have experienced a UFO sighting—often report a lapse in consciousness, or a period of time that has passed for which they cannot account. This lost period can be as brief as a few minutes or as long as a day or two. Note: If the last thing you saw before experiencing this type of blackout was the underside of a bar stool, you probably aren't a true abductee.

vivors abound—and they are bulging with accounts of human–alien sexual encounters or genetic experimentation. Besides, just one look at Al Gore should be enough to convince you that a race of Spock-like, emotionally stunted intellectuals really does walk among us.

## Know Your Extraterrestrials

The fact is, there are as many "types" of aliens as there are types of humans. I mean, there are nice ones and not-so-nice ones. You have Jesus Christ and you have Newt Gingrich. You know what I mean.

Anyway, you can insult most humanoids and live (hint: don't try this in a bingo hall), but it's not a good idea to make some silly faux pas when meeting a being from outer space for the first time. It might stick a probe into your gonads. And that's the best-case scenario. It's best to bone up on the alien "races" that make up the universe while you have the chance.

*The Grays:* These are the alien types most often depicted in movies. They are thin and short (from two to five feet tall), with humanoid body types and distinctly strange facial features (i.e., tiny black eyes, small or nonexistent noses, and slitlike mouths). They are considered to be at best amoral and at worst antagonistic toward human beings.

*The Blonds:* Similar in appearance to the Grays but with more human characteristics, the Blonds are generally friendly and helpful toward the humans they encounter.

*The Hairy Dwarfs:* Picture Herve Villechaize. Now picture him dipped in a bucket of pubic hair. Close enough.

*The Very Talls:* People seem to have trouble finding this type of alien. I can't imagine why. I'd check the NBA.

*Get in Condition.* James Marrs believes that, although no one can be certain of the aliens' ultimate plan for us, what we are seeing are the effects of a "human conditioning program" . . . and that the program is working *on us.*

Marrs explained his theory this way: "We are all being conditioned to accept the reality of extraterrestrial life. Let me give you an example. Back in the 1970s, scientists discovered what appeared to be a Stone Age tribe living in a remote area of the Philippines. For the first time, instead of us just rushing in with clothes and tools and Bibles and everything and saying 'Here, get civilized,' we finally showed a little bit of smarts and quarantined the whole area. Then we sent in a pool of scientists who would condition these people—actually get them used to the reality of modern human beings—so they could accept the researchers as a normal part of their lives.

> *Maybe this world is another planet's hell.*
> *—Aldous Huxley*

"For the first week or so, the researchers would simply sit within the villagers' view, but at a distance. The next week, they would move slightly closer—not close enough to interact, but within the villagers' notice. In a few days, perhaps they would move to a clearing. Some time after that, they might start to smile and wave, and so on. After a while the tribesmen began to get acclimatized to the scientists' presence. And they began to realize, Okay . . . these people are here. And by the time the scientists finally made contact, the villagers knew their visitors were neither enemies nor a threat.

"Anyway, I feel that we've been undergoing the same type of conditioning, except we're the villagers and the ETs are the visitors. And since polls show that most people accept the truth of intelligent life beyond Earth, they've gotten us pretty close to the point where most people could handle it if it was announced that, yes, there is life out there, and yes, it is making contact with us."

# 32

## The Men Who
## Mooned the World

*The Moon is essentially gray, no color.*
*It looks like plaster of Paris, like dirty beach sand*
*with lots of footprints in it.*
—JAMES LOVELL, ASTRONAUT

*H*mmm . . . that's interesting, isn't it? Here we were, romanticizing the lunar surface, and it turns out the Moon isn't really so different from the terrain of, say, the deserts of remote Nevada! Hey . . . that gives me an idea for a great movie. What if American astronauts never got any closer to the Sea of Tranquility on July 20, 1969, than they did to, say, a rudimentary soundstage in some remote wasteland? What if the whole lunar landing was nothing but an elaborately staged drama, filmed and presented as real to a space-obsessed world?

Are you thinking I should pitch that to some producer? I'm sorry to say a lot of theorists believe that that movie's already been pitched, developed, and produced. What's more, we've all seen it.

According to Bill Kaysing, former technical writer for Rockwell International and one of NASA's most vociferous and knowledgeable critics, we may believe that Neil Armstrong and Edwin "Buzz" Aldrin came back from the "Moon"

## Coincidence or Conspiracy?
## Are the Stars Out Tonight?
## Apparently Not.

"I think a future flight should include a poet, a priest, and a philosopher . . . we might get a much better idea of what we saw." That's what astronaut Michael Collins said after his trip to the Moon. But I think we'd save on personnel if we just included a decent photo retoucher.

Here's the deal: The Moon lacks any atmosphere that would block the view of the stars around it. Nevertheless, in photographs of the lunar sky, those billions and billions of stars Carl Sagan went on and on about are curiously absent. Why, in an environment that scientists agree would give us pathetic earthlings the most magnificent view of the star-spangled cosmos ever, does the background fade to black? And why have NASA's best and brightest been so tight-lipped about it?

Bill Kaysing suggests that although NASA was sure it could fool most of the people most of the time, a starry backdrop would never have passed muster with real astronomers. He also suggests that the lunar astronauts might have been paid for their silence with high-powered executive positions. Or, barring that, they may have been subjected to mind control to keep them quiet about where they have or have not been.

with a few bags of rocks and enough stirringly scripted speeches to ensure them a lifetime of speaker's fees. But if the cameras had captured the astronauts' real adventure, we would have been watching them simulating movement in one-sixth gravity (with cranes and wires. Hey—Peter Pan did it!), frolicking in some really bad lighting, and—according to some reports—cavorting with a few women imported from nearby Reno. The only things they were likely to "return to Earth" with were some really nasty hangovers and maybe a hickey or two.

While most Americans will-ingly joined the media-orches-trated frenzy of patriotic fervor the moment Armstrong made his giant leap from the steps of the lunar module into the moon-dust, the truth is that there were millions of observant skeptics who were watching the same scene in total disbelief. As Kaysing describes in his fascinat-ing book *We Never Went to the Moon: America's Thirty Billion Dollar Swindle!*, they had good reason to mistrust what they were seeing. Armstrong left deep footprints in the soft, plaster of Paris–like lunar surface. So why didn't the lunar module's thrusters blast module-size craters in the dust? Why did it appear that the astro-nots were lit from both sides simultaneously? Was the Moon the ultimate in ambient lighting?

### BEEN THERE, DONE THAT

Where do these clever Hollywood scriptwriters get their ideas? Apparently, from NASA! This theory is not only depict-ed in the 1971 James Bond film *Diamonds Are Forever*, it resurfaces as an ersatz flight to Mars in *Capricorn One*.

If this "Only a Paper Moon" scenario strikes you as pretty outrageous, consider this: in order to assure the public of its ongoing success, NASA would have had to fake all six Moon landings to the tune of some $25 billion. What could possibly motivate the space agency—and all the other agencies necessary to perpetuate such a hoax—to fake it? To put a clean end to the space race between the Soviet Union and the United States. Or

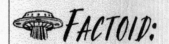

Even James Oberg, a space-flight operations engineer at Rockwell Interna-tional and Kaysing debunker, estimates that there are between 10 and 25 million Americans who doubt the reality of the lunar landing.

## Pie in the Sky

*In the late fifties, when I was at Rocketdyne, they did a feasibility study on astronauts landing on the Moon. They found that the chance of success was something like .0017 percent. In other words, it was hopeless. It's also well documented that NASA was often badly managed and had poor quality control. But as of '69, we could suddenly perform manned flight upon manned flight? With complete success? It's just against all statistical odds.*

—Bill Kaysing

to keep the billions of tax dollars NASA sucks in each year coming. But that possibility raises what may be a more ominous motivation. If space exploration were just a front, then the billions earmarked for NASA could be used to fund virtually any covert cause . . . like the overthrowing of unpopular governments, attempted assassinations on world leaders, or any other program they want us to pay for but not necessarily to know about.

But how about those blastoffs? The rocket boosters thrusting, the clouds of smoke and steam rising, Walter Cronkite reporting . . . we saw all that, didn't we? Sure we did. But the fact that a spacecraft is launched doesn't ensure its destination. Courses can be changed. Occupants can be jettisoned, then plucked safely from the sea. Or, if they're lucky, transported to the waiting arms of Reno showgirls and a well-earned vacation in the Nevada desert.

# 33

I'll See You
on the Dark Side
of the Moon

*O*f course, NASA's party line is that we have, in fact, planted our flag upon the surface of the Moon. They are also quick to add that we didn't find much there: just a few rocks . . . some really big craters. But haven't you wondered why we haven't returned to the satellite we claimed in 1969—if only to pillage and destroy, like good explorers? Haven't you wondered why NASA is investing its time, effort, and your money in an orbiting space station instead of in the establishment of a stationary base on a moon we have visited, where raw materials can be mined and supplies can be stockpiled? Could it be that the astronauts found a lot more than rocks on the lunar surface . . . and that what they found rocked their plans for colonization? Check it out.

You all know what NASA showed you: Neil Armstrong thumping around in the moondust, reveling in the exquisite and frightening solitude of a destination some 230,000 mean miles away from what he would call daily life. (I love that. *Mean* miles. Like the Long Island Expressway is so pleasant.)

Well, it turns out that that film may have been edited by the same people who chopped up the Zapruder film, possibly using the same knife and fork they used to botch JFK's autopsy. Because according to researcher Timothy Good—and a number of other theorists—the American astronauts were not alone on the lunar surface . . . nor were they welcome there.

According to several reports, both Neil Armstrong and Buzz Aldrin first saw UFOs shortly after the historic landing of Apollo 11. Otto Binder, a former NASA employee, claims that he and other ham radio buffs actually eavesdropped on NASA's communications with the crew—and that he picked up the following exchange:

NASA: *What's there? Mission Control calling Apollo 11. . . .*
APOLLO 11: *These "babies" are huge! Enormous! Oh, my God! You wouldn't believe it! I'm telling you there are other spacecraft out there, lined up on the far side of the crater edge. They're on the Moon watching us!*

In his book *Above Top Secret*, researcher Timothy Good further suggests that we were essentially thrown off the Moon by its inhabitants. Even the usually tight-lipped Neil Armstrong, asked to explain the United States' abandonment of its own plans for a lunar base, was quoted as saying, "It was incredible! Of course, we had always known there was a possibility [of intelligent life on the Moon]. The fact is, we were warned off! There was never any question then of a space station or moon city."

By now you're probably thinking this whole scenario could simply have been cooked up—that it's nothing more than a lunar "War of the Worlds." Think again. In 1979, Maurice Chatelain, former chief of communications systems, confirmed that Armstrong had reported seeing two UFOs on the rim of a crater. He described the situation as "common knowledge in NASA," though no one dared speak of it publicly for fear of a mass panic.

Nor were the Apollo astronauts the only flyboys to experience close encounters. Chatelain has said that nearly all Apollo and Gemini flights were followed by space vehicles of extraterrestrial origin. He even quipped that Mercury astronaut Wally Schirra used the code name "Santa Claus" to alert mission control to his UFO sightings.

But if the idea of an alien base on the far side of the Moon—or even the suggestion of intelligent life on the Moon—still seems a bit "out there" for you, consider this: Richard Hoagland, former science adviser to CBS News and a NASA consultant, has revealed photographic evidence of hundreds of "anomalies" on the lunar surface, including many believed to be the remains of massive, ancient alien glass structures. The photos, taken during the Apollo lunar missions, clearly show the architectural bones of massive, somewhat eroded lunar structures, including:

## Don't Get NASA-ty

The National Aeronautic and Space Administration is technically a civilian agency. You would think that that means it has a responsibility to report its findings to me and you, but NOOOOOOOO. Many of NASA's programs are funded with Defense Department dollars. The Defense Department is nothing more than the CIA in a five-sided building. And the CIA has been busy squelching UFO-related evidence for fifty years!

"The Shard": a towering, vertical construct that rises one and a half miles from the lunar surface

"The Castle": a complex edifice that is actually suspended miles above the surface of the Moon by what appears to be a cable

"The Bridge": a suspension bridge much like any you'd find on Earth (but without the tollbooth), built from a number of right-angle brackets, couplings, and a box-like framework suspended from an overarching span.

These photos are easily accessible. They can be viewed in a number of books (for example, *Extra Terrestrial Archaeology: Incredible Proof We Are Not Alone* by David Hatcher Childress) or pulled up on the World Wide Web. (Just type "lunar structures" or "lunar archeology" into your search engine and

Evidence abounds that the Earth's moon is indeed hollow—and somebody may very well be home. The maverick archaeologist David Hatcher Childress, who believes that the unexplained structures on the lunar surface are the vestiges of past civilizations, suggests that it is possible that the Moon continues to function as an alien base. In his fascinating and provocative book *Extra Terrestrial Archaeology,* he even proposes that the Moon might not be a solid mass at all but "a spaceship with an inner metallic-rock shell beneath miles of dirt and dust and rock."

Jim Marrs arrived at the same conclusion in *Alien Agenda,* where he explores what he calls "Spaceship Moon" theory and provides us with some shocking evidence that the Moon is much more than just a source of "mood lighting."

According to Marrs, in 1969, when the Apollo 12 lunar ascent stage fell back onto the surface of the Moon, seismic instruments indicated that the Moon reverberated like a bell for more than an hour. You don't have to be a physicist to know there would have been no such effect unless the orb were hollow. I know what you're thinking: you're thinking, Hey—Belz! Just because the Moon is hollow, that doesn't make it a spaceship! You're right. Dan Quayle has eyes, but that doesn't make him a potatoe. Er, potato. Anyway, the point is this: Nobody is sure just where the Moon came from. It isn't composed of the same elements as the Earth, so that blows any idea that it just broke off of its closest neighbor. And it isn't made of space debris. Since the Moon has just one-sixth the gravity of Earth, there would be no scientific reason for that much space junk to glom together. Is it so far-fetched, then, to consider the possibility that the Moon might have been produced by a superior race, then moved into Earth's gravitational pull? Isaac Asimov believed just that. And some scholars believe Aristotle described a prelunar time—before there was a moon in our sky. So isn't the spaceship moon theory worth a look?

Oh, by the way . . . the Moon happens to be a UFO hotspot. It is a site rife with unexplained lights, some of which have been captured on videotape by the space shuttle Discovery. A scientist named Jack Kasher tried to prove that the lights were ice crystals. Now he believes they are UFOs. But don't hold your breath until you get confirmation from NASA. They consider this kind of evidence to be "the Wrong Stuff."

you'll be up to your knees in evidence.) Take a few minutes to look them over. Then ask yourself: Which scenario is more likely? That these geometrically perfect, crystal monuments are the remnants of a previous—or perhaps an ongoing—civilization on the Moon? Or did Buzz Aldrin sculpt them out of Tang? Case closed.

## Get With the Programs

Contact with physically stunted, squinty-eyed, amoral beings with pallid complexions could be hazardous for human beings. Anyone who's ever shaken hands with Ross Perot knows that. So NASA and the CIA wouldn't keep information on alien encounters from us, would they? Hey, judge for yourself. How many of these research programs on UFO phenomena has NASA sent you direct-mail information on? How many have you seen on an infomercial? Or even heard about on the news? That's what I thought.

*Project Blue Book.* This United States Air Force program was implemented in 1952 to assess whether UFOs posed a threat to national security. What it proved was that the administrators of programs like this one posed a threat to national security. Though many UFO reports were gathered up by the Blue Book personnel, one investigator discovered that some dossiers—specifically those in which the UFO activity could not be explained or could cause public concern—were disappearing. It turns out that any suspicious reports (i.e., reports on legitimate UFOs) were being appropriated (read "hidden") by a higher authority. Project Blue Book was disbanded in 1969.

*Projects Moon Dust and Blue Fly.* Although the United States doesn't admit to playing around with flying saucer technology, these projects exist so that any nonexistent man-made space objects we don't produce can be covered after crashing by authorized personnel. Project Moon Dust, an officially classified agency, is also

> *Some agencies have a public affairs office. NASA is a public affairs office that has an agency.*
> —John Pike, Federation of American Scientists

engaged in the retrieval of space debris of foreign or unknown origin. This is only a guess, but I don't think we're talking about any flying saucers launched by the Pakistanis here.

*Project Pounce.* A top-secret project begun in 1953 to evaluate UFOs in order to gain more technological knowledge.

*Project Sigma.* A 1964 project that investigated ways to communicate effectively with aliens. This project was said to have reached its apex in 1964 when a United States Air Force officer allegedly met with two extraterrestrials in the New Mexico desert.

I don't know of any breakthroughs Project Sigma might have brought about in our communication with beings from other dimensions and times, but I understand that it has aided in our comprehension of Jesse Helms and other refugees from alternate universes.

## Conspiracy or Coincidence? Loose Lips Sink Space Programs

The lunar astronauts are notorious among journalists for their steadfast refusal to submit to interviews. Now let's think about this for a minute. We hear from the fifteen-minutes-of-fame crowd every day. But these men went to the Moon! Wouldn't they be NASA's biggest public relations assets? Why would these distinctly different individuals all decide to take a vow of silence? This has all the earmarks of a cover-up, but, like I said, don't go by me.

# 34

## Men in Black

Okay, we all saw the movie. There were Will Smith and Tommy Lee Jones and they were wearing some really nicely cut suits and they had this male-bonding thing going that was sort of like deer hunting only maybe a little slimier. (I don't know, I've never been deer hunting, okay? The Jews spent thousands of years hiding in the wilderness. So spending a weekend crouched behind a bush in the middle of the woods doesn't hold a lot of appeal for me.) And it was all kind of charming, wasn't it? You know . . . they walk alike, they talk alike, they even flash their little thingies alike . . . you could lose your mind! But the thing is, real Men in Black aren't hunting for aliens—they're hunting for the hapless schmoes who are unlucky enough to have a "glowing, cigar-shaped airship" pull into the parking space next to theirs at the Piggly Wiggly. And the way I hear it, people have lost their minds after an encounter with an MIB. Some have even lost their lives. And that's a plot twist that won't make it into anybody's "feel-good" movie about UFO-obsessed zombies.

## Black in the Dark Ages

We tend to think of MIBs as a recent phenomenon—or at least one that arose simultaneously with the advent of saucer activity in the 1940s and '50s. But that isn't true. According to Jim Keith, the best-selling author of *Casebook on the Men in Black,* reports of mysterious strangers dressed in black are woven throughout our history. But, Belz, you may argue . . . black is a slenderizing color. Okay. Whatever. But MIBs tended to pop up at moments of national uncertainty or crisis, so their presence was often noted. They also seemed to step out of the gloom just in time to offer philosophical guidance, opinion, or direction to some of our most prominent forebears. Here are a couple of examples:

• Jim Keith reports that Thomas Jefferson was accosted by a dark-complected stranger in a black cape while strolling in his garden one night. According to Keith, it was from this uninvited guest that Jefferson received the design for what became the Great Seal of the United States.

• Author Manly P. Hall, author of scads of books and articles on alchemy, secret societies, and other esoteric subjects, has suggested that just such a mysterious stranger was actually instrumental in the birth of America. In his metaphysical classic *The Secret Teachings of All Ages,* he describes a heated debate in the Old Philadelphia State House between colonial delegates who wished to make an open declaration of independence from the British king and those who did not. Just as the argument was reaching its height, a man known to no one in the company stepped forward and delivered a pro-independence speech so rousing and convincing that all argument was quelled. That evening, each of the delegates stepped forward to sign the Declaration of Independence. And the mysterious orator was never seen or heard from again.

 FACTOID:

### UNREALLY PLAZA

Researchers have suspected for years that the MIBs were active participants in the harrowing events in Dealey Plaza. Much of the suspicion has centered on a few of the weirdos on hand that day, most notably the dark-suited lurkers whom bystanders assumed to be Secret Service men. But the author of *Casebook on the Men in Black,* Jim Keith, reveals what might be an even more interesting twist.

A twenty-four-year-old man named Manuel Angel Ramirez was arrested in March 1967 by the Philippine National Bureau of Investigation for conspiring to assassinate then-President Ferdinand Marcos. Before questioning, the suspect was given a truth serum and put under hypnosis. In this state, Ramirez confessed that he had been recruited by a Special Operations Group of the CIA. He also claimed that one of his missions as a part of this group—an assassination—had been carried out in Dallas, Texas, on November 22, 1963. He also told investigators that the Kennedy hit had been organized by a black-haired man with "Oriental eyes" who drove a black car.

Of course, anyone close to a Kennedy murder investigator will tell you that assassination theory is a field replete with peculiar visitors and mysterious goings-on. Jim Marrs has heard from countless researchers who have been accosted by strangers and warned into silence. Marrs himself has been confronted by any number of curious men and unsolicited telephone "well-wishers" who offer him false information or attempt to lure him off a specific trail.

There are many conflicting theories surrounding the Men in Black, but what everybody seems to agree on is the first widely reported, post-UFO-sighting encounter with an MIB. On June 21, 1947, three days before pilot Kenneth Arnold's sighting and just short of two weeks before the crash at Roswell, Harold Dahl photographed six UFOs while traveling by boat in Puget Sound. While the crafts hovered above him, Dahl heard a sudden discharge. He looked up to see one of the crafts spewing metal and a viscous liquid onto the ocean and into Dahl's boat. The wreckage was heavy enough to cause an injury to Dahl's son and kill a pet dog that happened to be on board.

The next morning, Dahl says, he received an unexpected visitor: a peculiar-looking man in a black suit who was able to describe pre-

## MIB OR BELZER? CAN YOU TELL?

I know . . . it isn't always easy to tell paranormal visitors from regular human beings like, for instance, me. I hear that some conspiracy theorists even believe the current crop of MIBs actually based their distinctive look on mine. But I don't believe it. Black has always been considered a sophisticated, upscale look.

Anyway . . . can you tell the difference between The Belz and a weird-looking, witness-badgering automaton? I'd like to think so, but this comparison will tell the story. Here goes:

MIBs: Always dress in black.
Belzer: Black don't crack, baby.
MIBs: Usually described as wearing dark glasses.
Belzer: Me, too.
MIBs: Witnesses note their pallid or peculiar coloration.
Belzer: People who believe that everything is a conspiracy don't get out much, okay?
MIBs: Often described as looking "too perfect."
Belzer: Okay, I confess. Now I'll have to kill you.

cisely what Dahl had seen the day before as if he, too, had seen it from Dahl's vantage point. Then the man warned Dahl that if the story went any further there would certainly be recriminations.

The warning was not enough to dissuade Dahl. Having already told his boss, Fred Crisman, about the encounter, the two set about having the photographs developed and even finding a publisher. That's when things started to go wrong.

The photographs came back "fogged" and later disappeared altogether. Hotel-room chats among Dahl, Crisman, and Kenneth Arnold were leaked verbatim to the Tacoma papers, though no bug was ever discovered. A B-25 carrying samples of the wreckage from the Puget Sound encounter crashed en route to Hamilton Field in California. Two men were killed. And pilot Kenneth Arnold himself was nearly killed when the engine of his plane suddenly conked while landing at his home airport in Boise, Idaho. He later discovered that the fuel valve in his plane had been turned off.

Since then the veracity of Dahl's story has come under fire. Dahl himself reportedly admitted to Air Force personnel that his story was a hoax. But while some theorists have come to doubt the integrity of the Puget sighting, others believe that Dahl denied his experience for fear of further reproach by the mysterious Men in Black. I mean, what would you do? Most people would buckle under the threat of a missed meal.

If that story seems a little bizarre, it is—though not because MIB visitations rarely occur. Hundreds of people have gone on record with their encounters with real MIBs, and countless others have reported contacts within the context of UFO-contactee support or information groups. What makes Dahl's experience unique is that it so clearly describes what UFOlogists now identify as a "typical" MIB visitation— and that it has become a prototype for so many of the reports that followed.

So what constitutes a "typical" encounter with the Men in Black? For one thing, timing. MIBs generally come knocking just after a UFO sighting or some other alien-to-human contact. These MIBs, known in UFOlogists' circles as "silencers," typically threaten, hint at some undefined malevolence, or otherwise induce paranoia in recent UFO witnesses to ensure their total silence about what they have seen or experienced. When there is any doubt, MIBs can go so far as to steal notebooks, photographs, journals, or any other evidence of alien activity. They have also been known to dress in police blues or an intelligence officer's uniform, or just flash an official-looking badge in order to confiscate any evidence that needs suppressing.

Not that most people would dare to hang on to ET's autograph after a face-to-face enounter with one of these oddballs. MIBs are known for their distinctive and unnerving appearance. Which is to say that they're easier to pick out among the general population than Placido Domingo at a Public Enemy concert.

For one thing, MIBs don't go anywhere without their dark-framed glasses. And in the same circumstances, you wouldn't either. They are often described as having extremely slanted eyes. And when their eyes aren't slanted, they are said to be "bulging"—as if they had Ping-Pong balls implanted in their eye sockets. Their complexions are pasty and of a strange coloration. Although their faces have been described by some witnesses as "pallid," and by others "dark," almost all people who claim to have been approached by an MIB tell of an unsettling waxy, unreal, or "dead" look.

In fact, MIBs—by definition—would have some difficulty "looking alive." Those who have met them say they speak in a tinny, electronic-sounding, or machinelike monotone. They seem baffled by the accoutrements of human life, like ballpoint pens, food, and complicated tools, like forks. (Did I mention they tend to have tine marks in their faces?) And they tend to drive around in pristine black antique Cadillacs. I mean, how much more dead can you get than that? There are so many antique Cadillacs in retirement communities, the car is considered a "starter casket."

So who or what are the MIBs? And what's behind their conspiracy of silence? In a country that debates whether to feed hungry children, there are, of course, many theories.

Some researchers believe the Men in Black are aliens themselves and that their unique "Witness Suppression Program" is designed to maintain secrecy about their superior technology and their ultimate intentions on Earth. These theorists point to the MIBs' "otherworldly" behaviors—like spending a half an hour in a witness's living room marveling at the complex inner workings of a ballpoint pen—as evidence of an alien nature. I find that hard to believe. Can a guy who can't figure out which end of a spoon to stick in the food and which end to stick in his eye really be a member of a master race? Don't answer that if you're old enough to have lived through the presidency of Gerald Ford.

Anyway, if MIBs aren't spacemen, what are they? They could be a group of intelligence officers testing psychological-control techniques. (It's just plain mean to test on animals.) Or they could be a group of very human disinformation officers. Remember, the United States has been building its own flying saucers since World War II. And we know the government has managed to keep these advances secret by confusing our own airships with "alien" crafts. A covert group of vaguely malevolent Blues Brothers would further perplex the situation—and if they could silence witnesses using only extreme weirdness alone, so much the better. Last but not least likely, the MIBs might even be hoaxers. The fact is, we know only two things for sure about the Men in Black: that they are real, and that they are real strange.

# 35

## Black Choppers

*L*ook . . . up in the sky! It's a bird . . . no, it's a helicopter! And it's spraying a toxin that looks like a popular artificially colored gelatin dessert (I'm not worried about MIBs, but I have a healthy fear of trademark lawyers) all over me! Geez, I feel woozy. Hey . . . who should a person call in a case like this? Bill Cosby?

Knock yourself out, babe. Call anybody you want. Just don't waste your time calling the people who are supposed to deal with sudden and unexplained acts of a "higher power." FEMA (the Federal Emergency Management Agency) won't rescue you. And as for the choppers and the gelatin, well . . . rumor has it they already know all about them. . . .

For those of you who aren't privy to the darker side of the federal agencies that are supposed to help us (into a mass grave), the story begins in the early 1970s when, researchers agree, the skies began to fill with fleets of unmarked black helicopters. Nearly silent, totally unmarked, and fitted with tinted windows, the black helicopters were everything the casual observer would find easy to miss—except for their tendency to break every rule in the FAA regulation book.

First reported by ranchers in America's western states, the helicopters initially seemed more of an irritation than a threat. They would fly at very low altitudes—often unsettlingly low altitudes—in groups of two and three. Sometimes they would strafe the ground with a blindingly bright search beam or "buzz" herds of grazing animals below. But when concerned farmers began to lie in wait for these nocturnal nuisances, they discovered that the helicopters were for up a challenge. The choppers flew dangerously close to the ranchers' vehicles. They buzzed their houses. Some even fired on the fleeing farmers. And that was only the beginning.

On mornings following heavy helicopter activity, ranchers began to notice that one of their herd was missing. They would eventually discover the mutilated carcass of a cow in a remote area. On closer inspection they would find that the carcass was missing several body parts, usually the tongue, teats, and anus—and that these body parts had been removed with surgical precision. Now, let's think about this a minute. A cow has four stomachs, some strange and pendulous "baggage," and a chewing pattern indicative of advanced TMJ syndrome. Why bother maiming such an animal? Isn't it sort of redundant? Like blindfolding Earl Warren or tying Gerry Ford's shoelaces together? Anyway, the mysterious mutilations continue until this day, but with one additional strange twist: no footprints, tire tracks, or any other sign of human interference is ever found in the vicinity of the altered cows. It is as if old Bossy had been sucked off the face of the Earth by some airborne transport, given some unelective cosmetic enhancements, and gently lowered into its final resting place.

So what do you think about that? Makes you glad you aren't a cow, doesn't it? Well, don't get too excited. If anything, black chopper activity has increased since the 1970s. Unidentifiable helicopters have been reported in nearly every state of the union. And incidents related to helicopter activity have also "moved on up" into suburban areas. So they aren't just targeting cows anymore.

According to researcher and author Jim Keith, there have been thousands of reports of black helicopters spraying entire residential neighborhoods with an unidentified toxic mist. These chemicals have not only defoliated huge areas of once-wooded land, they have decimated area wildlife, killed birds and fish, deep-sixed family pets, and filled emergency rooms with coughing, retching men, women, and children who have come into contact with the poison. Witnesses also report being sprayed with a particularly nasty toxin that is delivered in gelatinlike globs. In *Black Helicopters II: The Endgame Strategy*, Jim Keith tells of a 1994 attack on the town of Oakville, Washington, population 665. Residents report that the tiny town was blanketed with the noxious goo six times in a three-week period. Many animals died. Humans who touched the material became instantly and violently ill. As one Oakville resident, Maurice Gobeil, put it, "I got sick, my wife got sick, my daughter; everybody who lives here got sick." And there are dozens upon dozens of towns just like Oakville from Maine to California. Are you still wondering why people in certain areas of the country are reporting unexplainable cancer clusters? Are you still wondering why there has been such an upsurge in respiratory illness? Are you still wondering why I live in France?

Just as in the case of the Men in Black, there are those who speculate that the black helicopters are of alien origin. Some have come forward to say that they have actually been abducted by the choppers and taken to a flying disk for examination—thus proving an extraterrestrial connection. Others theorize that because bovine plasma happens to be chemically similar to human blood, aliens may be using the cow parts to facilitate their ongoing research into alien–human hybridization. But toxic showers and defoliation techniques aren't really a part of the alien repertoire, are they? Those techniques were perfected much closer to home.

In case you're thinking, Oh, sure . . . Belzer's government-bashing again, let me remind you that the United States has a long and illustrious history of using its own people as laboratory rats. In 1977, Pentagon officials were forced to admit that they had subjected their fellow Americans to 239 biological-warfare tests between 1949 and 1969. Although some insiders claim that the actual number of such tests was a lot closer to a thousand, everybody agrees that millions of innocent men, women, and children were exposed to a veritable all-you-can-breathe buffet of biological killers—including various deadly

## Two Years at Camp and I Feel Like a New Dissident!

In case you're one of those Doubting Thomases who simply can't accept the idea that the U.S. government would ever incarcerate innocent American citizens (I guess you aren't a Japanese émigré, are you?), listen to what Jim Marrs had to say on the subject:

"No doubt about it, FEMA's got these detention centers for 'dissidents.' The only thing is, who decides who the dissidents are? One of the criteria for a dissident is someone who poses opposition to a military operation abroad. So if the Pentagon decides they are going to bomb Bosnia and we oppose it, we're dissidents. They can round us all up and put us in the camp.

"And I'll tell you, these camps exist. I've been to one down here in Texas. It just had acre after acre of mobile homes sitting empty. It looked like a used mobile-home lot.

"I didn't go in—I just went as far as the front gate—but I know some people who went in to take a closer look. They said it looked deserted. But it must have some sophisticated surveillance equipment, because the next thing they know, here come some guys with guns in jeeps to run them off.

"So, what do these camps tell me? They tell me that the government is preparing for something. I don't know what it is, and it's possible that not even they know what it is. Just contingency planning. A buildup toward an event."

bacteria, known carcinogens like zinc cadmium sulfide, countless poisons, and even radiation—for twenty years *by their
own government*! Do you think these people might mutilate
a cow? Shit! As you read this, they're stringing their tennis
rackets with all of those cow anuses. Don't even think about
the tongues.

But the scenario might be even more chilling than that.
Jim Keith and other chopper investigators believe that the
helicopters have already been used in armed combat against
innocent Americans—in Waco, Texas, where they assisted in
the immolation of David Koresh and the Branch Davidians,
and in Idaho, where they provided surveillance for FBI agents
in the debacle at Ruby Ridge. They further suggest that the
unmarked fleet now hovering over whatever state you're in is
a grim foreshadowing of the dictatorial police state you will be
living in in the not-too-distant future.

The theory goes like this: In 1974, a year characterized by
the ongoing Watergate affair, impeachment hearings against
Richard Nixon, and the kidnapping of Patricia Hearst ("My
God, Mommy, they've kidnapped a socialite. What's next? The
knifepoint cornrowing of the Junior League?"), Governor
Ronald Reagan of California began to panic. What would happen if the government of the United States collapsed? What
mayhem would ensue if a major city were taken hostage by a
rioting underclass? And how far up in the political hierarchy
did a fellow have to go to get a decent nap? Reagan requested
a study. Later that year, FEMA—the Federal Emergency Management Agency—was formed.

You know FEMA, don't you? Oh, sure you do. Anybody
who watches the ongoing disaster-epic known as the network
news knows FEMA. If your town floods, FEMA is the agency
that sees to it you have enough water. And if a hurricane flat-
tens the county, it is FEMA that oversees the flow of federal
rehabilitative funds. But FEMA has a side that is not so well
known—and not so benevolent. As Jim Keith reveals in *Black
Helicopters II,* "FEMA's latitude for control is vast." Among its
many powers are:

- the authority to suspend freedom of speech,
- the authority to take over electrical and other power systems,
- the authority to take full control of food sources, including farms,
- the ability to form work brigades of citizens,
- the authority to take over airports, railways, waterways, and all transportation systems, public or private, and, my personal favorite,
- *the authority to take over the executive functions of the government.*

Shocking, isn't it? Sort of like finding out that the man who threw up on the emperor of Japan is going to negotiate our next trade agreement with them. ("You throw up on my leg? Now I'm going to fuck you up economically!") Okay, maybe that's a bad example. But bear with me. There's more.

In May of 1992, police and military personnel from the United States, Canada, and the Soviet Union gathered in Alaska for a jolly little fete called "Police 2000." The goal of this cabal was to literally gather the forces into a "transnational police organization for the coming global village." This international police force would unite agents now operating as National Security Administration, Drug Enforcement Agency, CIA, FBI, and local law-enforcement officials into one body, under the aegis of . . . you guessed it! FEMA.

And what does all of this have to do with the choppers? Current sightings seem to center around twenty-three detention camps set aside for use by the Federal Emergency Management Agency. Researchers estimate that those camps can house a minimum of 700,000 people like you and I. (Never pay for books like this with credit cards. *Never*.)

So, what do you think? Is there an emergency in the making? Who are you gonna call? Guess again.

# 36

# Face It . . .
# There's a Face on Mars

*O*n August 23, 1993, NASA's anxiously awaited probe, the $1 billion Mars Observer, mysteriously "ceased operating" just as it began its entry into the orbit of the Red Planet. Shortly thereafter, NASA graciously

*If you want a picture of the future, imagine a boot stomping on a human face—forever.*
—*George Orwell*

stepped forward to inform the world that the Observer had ceased observing, that it was finished, kaput, DOA. Most people accepted that story. I didn't. And neither did tens of thousands of investigators and space-ophiles all over the world who believe that the probe is still out there, taking pictures of stuff NASA doesn't want us to see, and beaming them into the hands of the select few NASA has deemed worthy. Oh, come on, Richard, you're probably saying. I know what an airless, life-crushing wasteland is. I've changed planes in Arizona! So what could there possibly be to take pictures of on Mars? In a word, plenty.

It might surprise you to know that early astronomers considered Mars to be the planet in our solar system most likely to support life. (I mean, other than Earth, of course. Here every type of vermin thrives.) Those astronomers believed that the surface of the Red Planet was covered with canals and because of those conduits, Mars was a garden spot, replete with vegetation. Needless to say, canals don't dig themselves. I noticed that when I was in the Army, shortly after somebody handed me a shovel. Consequently, astronomers at the turn of the century were convinced that there were intelligent beings on Mars who built not only the canals but other structures, like bridges, over them (see quote on page 203). To them, Mars was like Vegas after the Mob came in. Civilized. Bustling. A planet that would be perfect if only someone had thought to put in a sphinx and a facsimile of the pyramid of Giza and maybe a working volcano or two.

And everybody was happy to think all that until 1969, when NASA's Mariner probes began to transmit the first photos of the surface of Mars. That's when it became apparent that Mars was not like Vegas at all. It was bleak. It was rocky. And there was no sign of the canals, or the bridges, or life in any form . . . until 1971, when Mariner 9 captured some rather peculiar images.

While photographing an area called the Elysium Quadrangle, Mariner passed over and photographed several pyramid-shaped formations. But were they natural formations or man-made structures? Richard Hoagland, who identified and

## Lost in Space?

Can something the size of a Mars probe just disappear into space? NASA says yes. Jim Marrs says different: "How silly is that? With radar and with telescopes and with all the stuff we've got, I guarantee they know every little piece of space junk that's orbiting the Earth. They know, for instance, that there are something like 1,200 individual items orbiting the Earth, including a screwdriver that was dropped by Russian cosmonauts. They can't just lose something the size of a spacecraft! What do you mean you've lost it? Where has it gone?"

catalogued the looming structures on the lunar surface, believed they might have been evidence of a Martian civilization. Other scientists wondered whether there might be a connection between the pyramid on Mars and the five-sided monument at Giza, Egypt. Were the two pyramids geometrically similar? If there were a pyramid on Mars, could there also be a sphinx like the one in Giza? And if you hung around long enough on the Elysium Quadrangle, would somebody come by and offer you a ride on a really nasty, molty-looking camel for just a couple of dinars? They didn't have to wonder long.

### MARTIANS BUILD TWO IMMENSE CANALS IN TWO YEARS
### *Vast Engineering Works Accomplished in an Incredibly Short Time by Our Planetary Neighbors*
—New York Times *headline, 1911*

In the summer of 1976, the Viking orbiter caused an unprecedented sensation when, while traversing the area known as "Cydonia," it transmitted photographs of what appeared to be an enormous, sculpted face staring up from the Martian surface. Since the orbiter was known to be traveling some thousand miles above Mars, such a structure would have to be what is known technically as a whopper. And it was. The face was estimated to be 1,500 feet high, 1.2 miles wide, and more than a mile and a half long.

Of course, you know and I know that just because a piece of evidence happens to be the size of, say, a plaza in Dallas doesn't mean those in authority will acknowledge its existence. NASA dismissed the structure as a trick of the light. (What else could they say? Weather balloons don't fly that high.) But images taken by the Viking probe always depicted the face, even when the sun was at a different angle. And when two computer scientists, Vincent DiPeitro and Gregory Molenaar, digitally enhanced the Viking images, it simply showed the truth of the matter in starker relief. The face wasn't a trick of light or the result of natural erosion: it was not only perfectly symmetrical but painstakingly detailed. Its eyes had pupils, sculpted teeth were visible between its lips, and it appeared to be wearing a cap with a huge X right in the

## Coincidence or Conspiracy?
## (All together, now . . . ) Oops . . .
## There Goes Another Faulty Mars Probe!

The path to Mars is strewn with so much wreckage, pretty soon we'll be able to throw a rug over it and walk to the Red Planet. But in case you've been too obsessed with presidential assassinations and the marginalization of three decades of eyewitnesses to notice, here is a rundown of the space race to oblivion:

*October 1960:* The USSR launches Korabl 4 and Korabl 5, both believed to be Mars probes. Each fails in Earth orbit.

*October 1962:* The USSR launches Korabl 11. (If you're wondering what happened to Korabls six through ten, they were melted down and turned into steel-toed high heels for stylish Soviet factory workers.) It crashes back to Earth five days after blastoff.

*November 1962:* Korabl 13 is launched and crashes the next day.

*November 1964:* The United States launches Mariner 3. The vehicle experiences a launch failure and enters solar orbit.

*May 1971:* On May 5, America's Mariner 8 blasts off but fails to achieve orbit. Two days later, the Soviets launch Kosmos 419. It fails to leave Earth orbit. I guess this orbit thing can be pretty tricky.

*November 1971:* Mars 2 and its lander crash on Mars.

*July 1976:* Viking 1 and Viking 2 successfully land on Mars. Viking 2 ceases communications in April of 1980. Viking 1 follows suit in November of 1982.

middle of it! Okay, forget the X part, but the face was definitely depicted as wearing some sort of a headdress, which some experts describe as the type worn by Mayan or Egyptian royalty, so I ain't talkin' a babushka here.

*July 1988:* The USSR tries again, this time with twin probes: Phobos 1 and 2. Contact with Phobos 1 is lost less than two months later when, due to a computer error, the probe receives an erroneous "suicide" command from Earth. Whoo! Let's keep the Russians off of our "buddy lists," okay? Phobos 2 becomes incommunicado as of March 1989.

*August 1993:* The United States loses contact with the Mars Observer.

*November 1996:* Russia's $300 million Mars 96 probe suffers rocket failure after launch and crashes into the Pacific Ocean.

You're probably thinking, Hey—who cares if NASA is splattering zillions of dollars across the countryside every decade. I'm still working! I can pay for these probes and lots more of 'em! But that's not the point.

Richard Hoagland nearly had to hog-tie and torture NASA officials before the space agency would agree to add the mysterious Cydonia region to the Observer's itinerary. Consequently, some investigators feel that the timing of the probe's disappearance—on the eve of what would have been significant and public revelations about Cydonia—might be a little too coincidental. Others—myself included—suspect a genuine cover-up.

What do you think? Was the Mars Observer stopped short by unforeseeable circumstance—like our thirty-fifth president? Is a hangar full of nothing being kept under lock and key at Wright-Patterson Air Force Base? Think about it. Then get back to work. NASA needs your tax dollars.

But wait! There's more. . . . the photographs also revealed some additional "anomalies" just a few miles from the sphinx. These include a five-sided pyramid nearly two miles wide at the base and what Richard Hoagland believes are the remnants of a city complex meticulously laid out so that all three structures—face, pyramid, and town—form a perfect equilateral triangle.

Holy Cheops, Batman! What does it all mean? Hey, don't ask me. NASA's got all the answers here. It just happens that they're wrong. But I'll tell you what it *could* mean. It could mean that the same race or type of beings built both the pyramids and sphinxes of Egypt and Mars. That would mean that these happy builders just packed up their chisels one day and moved from Mars to Egypt. Or that they abducted some human specimens from Earth, transported them to Mars, showed them how to build a really big face and some other stuff, then plopped them back down in Egypt. One scenario would make us the Martians' students; the other would make us their direct descendants. I suggest that you choose the one that allows you to sleep without the use of prescription drugs.

Or, if you want to get angry, consider what the case of the face on Mars suggests about the government's tendency to cover, distort, conceal, and obscure information in general. For more than two decades, NASA has been officially silent on the issue of the Martian structures. In fact, personnel at the space agency have shown an almost inhuman lack of interest in or concern for the matter since the day Viking dropped Frame 35A72—the frame displaying the face in all its uneroded glory—into their laps in 1976. In fact, they have not only stubbornly resisted requests from scientists around the world calling for further investigation of the Cydonia region, they may even have sabotaged subsequent Mars probes just to keep from substantiating the existence of (now, get this) the face, the pyramids, and an entire civilization *they discovered themselves!* Did you hear that? These are not just photos taken with a disposable camera by a vacationing *Jerry Springer Show* regular. NASA took these pictures! And they're not even blurry!

So although they certainly never intended to do so, NASA has inadvertently provided the world with visual, seeing-is-believing evidence of something they steadfastly deny: the possibility of life on other planets. Nevertheless, they continue to marginalize, discredit, and harass those who accept the validity of what they themselves have found! And people wonder why wackos like me keep dredging up the possibility that the Kennedy assassination was a cover-up? Do you think that, if the FBI put sharpshooters in the windows of the Texas School Book Depository and told them to shoot at a target moving through the plaza at eleven miles per hour and they couldn't do it, those test results would be common knowledge? Well, that's just what happened. And the test results are not common knowledge. No evidence that might upset the status quo will ever be known. And if you don't believe me, go ask Dorothy Kilgallen.

But, Richard, you're undoubtedly kvetching . . . Life on other planets could have a big impact on our own lives. Like an *impact* . . . as in Ba-BOOM. Why would our government prefer it if we didn't know? This is an easy one. Remember back in 1938 when Orson Welles did a little radio skit called "War of the Worlds"? Well, trust me on this: the Defense Department, the military, and the intelligence wanks remember. People were yelling, screaming, and panicking in the streets. They weren't going to listen to any cop telling them to calm down and return to their homes. They weren't going to obey any civil, legal, or even papal official telling them where they could and couldn't go. And they weren't concerned about whether their taxes were paid up, either. Would that scenario be any different if we learned that Martians were in a position to land in Yankee Stadium tomorrow? There. You answered your own question. God didn't make no little green men and it don't rain in Indianapolis in the summertime. End of story.

Or at least it *would* be if conspiracy stories really had ends. But they don't have ends, they just have curious detours—and this one is no exception. In January 1998, NASA announced that a fossilized microbe found in a Martian meteorite led them to believe that (gasp!) there was evidence that what we think of as life might have existed on Mars. While the world focused on this microscopic find, conspiracy theorists pointed to the bigger picture. Microbe? NASA is willing to make much of the implications of a microbe while steadfastly refusing to see a face that's a mile and a half long and a pyramid that's two miles wide? Why? I'll tell you why. Because the microbe allows the space agency to condition us, much the same way Jim Marrs described the conditioning of that tribe in the Philippines. With Cydonia a matter of public record, NASA knows it is just a matter of time before they are forced to admit the huge truth of extraterrestrial life. By beginning the story at the microbial level, NASA buys itself unlimited time to build a story we can live with, molecule by molecule. It begins with Hey . . . we found a microbe! Then, maybe ten years later, it's Wow . . . get a load of this organism! The next thing you know, they've found a face, a pyramid, a place where a one-eyed, one-horned flying purple people-eater can get a fifteen-minute lube job, and a great venue for Chita Rivera, but nobody gives a shit because it's taken them a hundred and fifty years to tell the story.

## 37

# Embrace Me,
# You Sweet
# Embraceable Anthropoid

Who hasn't dug out the little black book on a Friday night, scanned the yellowed list of the same old names and numbers, and thought, Why can't I ever meet someone who is truly unique, someone so special she seems to set everything aglow . . . you know, like the fish near Three Mile Island? Why doesn't a certain entity, er, *someone* drop into my life, communicate his desire with a series of irresistible metallic buzzes and clicks, and join me in a sexual lollapalooza that will leave me scarred and suffering from radiation sickness and panting for more?

Who hasn't thought those things? I'll tell you who hasn't thought those things. The woman who caught the compound eye of an amorous giant grasshopper—only to discover her new friend had only one thing on its mind. The adolescent who began having intercourse at age thirteen—with a withered crone who mysteriously materialized in his bedroom. And anybody else who happens to be among the thousands of people who claim to have had sexual congress with a being from another planet.

I have to tell you, I love the term "sexual congress." It really tells the story, doesn't it? Well, as it turns out, so does the term "universal love." Indeed, reports of hot dates with aliens have become so common, entire industries seem to be growing up around the issue. There are regression therapists who specialize in helping ETs' exes relive their experiences and researchers who can't keep up with incoming reports. For all I know, there are designers hard at work right now on a line of condoms that will fit some rather oddly shaped "probes."

You're probably thinking that sex with aliens must be a relatively recent development, sort of like that gerbil thing in the eighties or the cigar thing in the nineties. The fact is, it isn't. People have been getting it on with grays, insectoids, and aliens who have assumed human form almost as long as they've been doing it with melons, battery-powered devices, and themselves. In fact, the first widely published case of sexual abduction took place only about ten years after the dawn of the modern UFO era—and it is a classic.

It was 1957 in São Paolo, Brazil. (And no, it still *isn't* 1957 in Brazil. Don't be such an arrogant American.) Antonio Villas Boas, a farmer, was out plowing his field when he was overcome by a dazzling light that, Boas said, looked like a "bright red star." Curious, Boas attempted several times to approach the source of the light, but it moved away from the farmer each time. He went home and reported the experience to his brother.

When Boas went out to plow again the following night, the "star" showed itself again. But this time it did not move away. It descended. When it got close enough for Boas to identify it as an egg-shaped airship, the farmer began to freak. He turned his tractor and attempted to flee, but the tractor—which had been running perfectly—suddenly stalled. The next thing he knew, he was overtaken by four small, grayish beings, dragged aboard the spacecraft, and forcibly stripped.

Whew! Hot stuff, huh? Well, listen to this. Boas was given a sponge bath with a clear, thick liquid. Then he was taken to another room, seated on a "strangely humped couch," and left alone to await his fate. He didn't wait long. Clouds of acrid gray smoke filled the room, and Boas was sickened by the vapors. He vomited on the floor. But when he struggled back to his feet, he found himself alone with a naked woman who had, as Boas described it, the most beautiful body he had ever seen. That was the good news. The bad news was that his companion also had large slanted eyes, almost no nose or lips, and Crayola-red pubic hair. Nevertheless, he managed to buck up, and before night was through he had had not one but two very close encounters. And he apparently pleased his partner, too. After collecting some sperm samples (that passes for afterplay on Alpha Centauri), she pointed mysteriously to her abdomen (as if hinting at a blessed event to come), then skyward. (In other words, don't bother sending any child support. Visitation is not an option.)

But was it as good for Boas as it was for the rest of us pathetic souls who skipped ahead to this chapter? Actually, Boas said it would have been better if his partner hadn't been growling and barking like an animal throughout the tryst. And he probably would have come away with a

### FACTOID:

**IT'S BEEN A BLASTOFF, BABE**
A 1992 Roper Poll indicated that at least 2 percent of the population—or more than five million Americans—claims to have been abducted by aliens.

better impression if he hadn't developed a raging case of radiation sickness shortly thereafter. Now, there's a disease that can make a "burning discharge" seem attractive.

Frankly, I don't think the drink has been mixed that could take the edge off of Boas's experience for me. But what can we learn from out-of-this-world experiences like this? Believe it or not, experts have compiled a list of the characteristics that mark extraterrestrial sex. According to Dr. Gregory Little, the author of *Grand Illusions: The Spectral Reality Underlying Sexual UFO Abductions, Crashed Saucers, Afterlife Experiences, Sacred Ancient Sites, and Other Enigmas* (whew! I could "do" a whole battalion of ETs in the time it takes to read that subtitle!), sexual abductions fall into three basic categories. They are:

🛸 *Gray's Anatomy.* This is my term for sexual experiences involving the short, ashen, almost traditional-looking aliens known as the "grays." Grays are pretty much asexual. That means they're in it to gather samples, not get you off. Consequently, if you're on a date with a gray, you might be probed or stuck with a needle but you probably won't be screwed stupid. Few female grays and even fewer males engage in what we think of as intercourse.

🛸 *Intergalactic Buggery.* This is sex with the reptilian, mantislike, or otherwise insect-type beings from other planets. Dr. Little offers few details of these encounters, though he does let us know that the genitalia of these creatures is "cold as ice." You'll probably be pleased, as I am, to know that these beings often have intercourse with the humans they pick up. Oy. Get me to the proctologist.

🛸 *Getting in Shape.* Some aliens can change shape at will. Sometimes these shape-changers thoughtfully transform themselves into tall blond humanoids with blue eyes before slapping the make on some unsuspecting *Homo sapiens.* I should be so lucky.

If you're getting the impression that alien sex has something for everybody, well . . . you're right. Let's say you're the uptight type who needs a drink or two before you're comfortable getting down and dirty with, say, a centipede. Aliens have been known to offer many of their sexual partners a friendly drink—and best of all, these concoctions might not even be connected to the postcoital rashes, sores, and cancers that often plague aliens' paramours. Into geriatric sex? You're in luck! Shape-changers have been known to adopt the guise of white-haired old women with deeply wrinkled faces. I'm all atingle just thinking about it. And if you like a sexually assertive succubus, one that is not afraid to grab the specimen by the cahungas, well . . . let's just say if you've come to the Pleiades looking for love, you've come to the right spot! Aliens

 *FACTOID:*

### ET WILL GET YOU TWENTY

You may be asking yourself: Hey . . . what's so wrong with a little interplanetary nookie? If my partner and I can overlook petty differences like ice-cold genitals, eight legs, or Hairy Dwarfism (figures, doesn't it? Other people get thoughtful aliens who transform themselves into Nordic-looking masseuses named Svenga. . . . Not me. I get Billy Barty after Rogaine), isn't this a private matter between two consenting what-evers? Don't be so sure.

In 1982, a little-known law was passed by the U.S. Congress that effectively made contact—including sexual contact—between humans and extraterrestrials illegal. Known as the "ET Exposure law," this statute authorized the quarantine and detention of (1) any person known to have entered the atmosphere of a celestial body other than Earth, (2) any earthling known to have "touched directly or been in proximity to any person, property, animal, or other form of life or matter who or which has been extra-terrestrially exposed." (Confused? Let me simplify for you. If he gives an address in light-years, or if she can accurately be described as a "life-form," your honey is prob-ably "extraterrestrially exposed." Got that? Good.) Quarantine could last as long as the National Aeronautic and Space Administration deemed necessary. Detention could commence without any of the usual foreplay, like a trial.

Considering that you could grab the U.S. Congress by the short and curlies and twist and they still would never admit that UFOs are real and aliens exist, this is pret-ty interesting stuff. Of course, NASA explained these issues all away by suggesting that this law was meant to apply only to astronauts returning to Earth who needed to be quarantined and tested for strange viruses. But that doesn't mean a civilian couldn't be carted off or detained indefinitely for reporting a close encounter. Or even the suspicion of one.

If you've been making the beast with two backs with something that might be a, well . . . an actual beast, you'll be happy to learn that this law was stricken from the books in 1991—but that doesn't mean there isn't a local ordinance against coitus intergalacticus. Before I guzzled any strange liquids or even chatted up some strange six-foot grasshopper, I would check with my local police department. It's bet-ter to be safe than sorry. Besides, now that Jack Ruby is gone, small-town cops are aching for some entertainment.

can be very hot, baby. So hot that one man, who was being badgered for nightly sex by one particularly horny female alien, forced himself to masturbate each night before retiring just so he would not be able to muster an erection when the alien turned up later on.

By the way, if you're thinking about having sex with an alien but you're concerned about the potential spiritual consequences of such an exploit (if I had a probe in my ass and grasshopper genitalia against my thigh, I know it's the first thing I'd be thinking about!), rest assured that even the Pope himself wouldn't have a problem. Experts agree that no matter what the position, no matter what the orifice, the aliens are collecting genetic material from their paramours. So they go for procreation, not recreation. And that makes it okay!

# 38

# The End of the Line

*I*t's not easy to end this kind of a book. I see conspiracy everywhere I look. I believe that history—past and current—is just a collection of accepted lies. So whether I'm looking at some biography based on accepted truth or today's *New York Times*, I see a conspiracy.

But maybe that's why I decided that the best place to end this book is with this theory, which addresses the big lie-in-the-sky the government insists on maintaining about aliens as well as the historical subject that still fascinates me most: our handsome, vigorous president who died young but, through the miracle of single-bullet ballistics, didn't leave a good-looking corpse.

> *Joyous distrust is a sign of health. Everything absolute belongs to pathology.*
> —*Friedrich Nietzsche*

For years, some theorists have suggested that Kennedy was taken out not because of the Bay of Pigs, or his war on organized crime, or because he dissed big bankers and billionaires, or even because he didn't ask for a bubble top on the Lincoln on

## THE PARANOIA RAP

Everything is a conspiracy.
Everything is.
Everything is a conspiracy.
Everything is.
JFK and LBJ,
RFK and Edgar J.,
FBI and CIA
MTV and VH1,
CSPAN 2 and CSPAN 1,
ABC and CBS,
NBC and all the rest,
Missing stars, the face on Mars,
Where's the Secret Service? In
  some bar!
Jack Ruby's past, the Roswell
  crash,
We've got Oswalds up the ass,
CNN and HBO,
Disney Channel, don't you know?
UFOs and Jackie Ohhhh!

November 22, 1963, but because he knew too much about UFOs. Not long ago, a purportedly top-secret CIA memorandum suggesting that JFK knew UFOs were real and shared that knowledge with Marilyn Monroe made the rounds at conventions. It was the hit of the show. Nevertheless, many serious researchers wrote it off as a very fringe idea with very little credibility . . . until now.

During my recent conversation with Jim Marrs, Jim described a document that had been given to him by two very reliable sources describing the scene at the Roswell crash site and also the wreckage found nearby at Socorro, New Mexico. The document described the wreckage as not belonging to any known military purpose and revealed that the bodies of several aliens had been removed from the site. Marrs also told me that the document was clearly circulated at the highest levels. He described it as "marked all over" by a veritable Who's Who of political and military honchos. Well, as provocative as each of those details might be, Marrs clearly saved the most compelling for last. Because at the end of the report the writer mentions that all of this information was shared with—guess who!—Senator John F. Kennedy.

According to this document, Kennedy was informed of these developments by someone in the office of the Secretary of the Air Force. If that is true—and there is little reason to doubt it, since JFK served as a young ensign with Naval Intelligence and also because he moved socially and professionally within these rarefied circles—it means that John Kennedy did, indeed, know the truth about our interplanetary visitors at the time of his death.

A question that was almost impossible to imagine can now be asked with a straight face: Was JFK snuffed to keep him quiet about UFO activity on Earth? And if so, couldn't the CIA have solved the problem by passing out exploding cigars to the aliens? You know. "Here you go, ET . . . have a Havana. Fidel had a blast with them!" Who knows? But if these scenarios seem as plausible as the single-bullet theory to you, my work is done here.

> *If you shut up the truth and bury it in the ground, it will grow and gather to itself such explosive power that the day it bursts through it will blow up everything in its way.*
> —*Émile Zola,* J'Accuse

# Acknowledgments

*I* acknowledge gratefully the invaluable diligence, patience, and utter grace with which my brilliant colleague Barbara Lagowski assisted me on *UFOs, JFK, and Elvis.*

I am especially moved by and appreciate Jim Marrs's generosity in talking with me and sharing some of his vast knowledge on these fascinating subjects.

Special thanks to Sandra Martin, my agent, Leslie Meredith, my editor, and Eric Gardner, my manager. My thanks also go to Kevin Rooney and Martin Olsen for their help, support, and friendship.

*M*any of you have probably asked yourselves: if I suddenly hit the big time, how would I spend my time? Basking on the Riviera? Ordering the help around? Debating the health risks of cigars with an intern in a windowless hallway? What I've done is read every book, magazine, publication, etc. on these pages and more. I know how to live, babe.

## Conspiracy, General Info, and Tons o' Fun

Moench, Doug. *The Big Book of the Unexplained*. New York: Paradox Press, 1997.

Moench, Doug, and Over 40 of the World's Top Comic Artists. *The Big Book of Conspiracies*. New York: Paradox Press, 1995.

*The Unexplained*. New York: Paradox Press, 1997.

Vankin, Jonathan, and John Whalen. *The 60 Greatest Conspiracies of All Time*. New York: Barnes & Noble Books, 1995.

## JFK

Benson, Michael. *Who's Who in the JFK Assassination.* New York: Citadel Press, 1993.

Crenshaw, Charles M., M.D. *JFK: Conspiracy of Silence.* New York: Signet, 1992.

David, Jay, ed. *The Weight of the Evidence: The Warren Report and Its Critics.* New York: Meredith Press, 1968.

Davis, John H. *The Kennedy Contract: The Mafia Plot to Assassinate the President.* New York: McGraw-Hill, 1993.

Duffy, James P., and Vincent L. Ricci. *The Assassination of John F. Kennedy.* New York: Thunder's Mouth Press, 1992.

Fetzer, James H., Ph.D., ed. *Assassination Science, Experts Speak Out on the Death of JFK.* Chicago: Catfeet Press, 1998.

Flammond, Paris. *The Kennedy Conspiracy.* New York: Meredith Press, 1969.

Fonzi, Gaeton. *The Last Investigation.* New York: Thunder's Mouth Press, 1993.

Ford, Gerald. *Portrait of the Assassin.* New York: Simon and Schuster, 1965.

Garrison, Jim. *On the Trail of the Assassins: My Investigation and Prosecution of the Murder of John F. Kennedy.* New York: Signet, 1990.

Griffith, Michael T. *Compelling Evidence: A New Look at the Assassination of President Kennedy.* Grand Prairie, TX: JFK Lancer Productions and Publications, 1996.

Groden, Robert J., and Harrison Edward Livingstone. *High Treason, The Assassination of President John F. Kennedy: What Really Happened.* New York: The Conservatory Press, 1989.

Groden, Robert J. *The Killing of a President.* New York: Viking Studio Books, 1993.

Hepburn, James. *Farewell America.* Vaduz, Liechtenstein: Frontiers, 1968.

Hubbard-Burrell, Joan. *What Really Happened?* Spring Branch, TX: Ponderosa Press, 1992.

Hurt, Henry. *Reasonable Doubt.* New York: Holt Rinehart & Winston, 1986.

Kantor, Seth. *The Ruby Cover-Up*. New York: Kensington, 1992.

La Fountaine, Ray and Mary. *Oswald Talked*. Gretna, LA: Pelican, 1996.

Lane, Mark. *Rush to Judgment*. New York: Holt Rinehart & Winston, 1966.

Lane, Mark. *Plausible Denial: Was the CIA Involved in the Assassination of JFK?* New York: Thunder's Mouth Press, 1992.

Lifton, David. *Best Evidence: Disguise and Deception in the Assassination of John F. Kennedy*. New York: Signet, 1992.

Livingstone, Harrison Edward. *Killing Kennedy*. New York: Carroll & Graf, 1995.

Livingstone, Harrison Edward. *Killing the Truth*. New York: Carroll & Graf, 1993.

Livingstone, Harrison Edward, and Robert J. Groden. *High Treason*. New York: Carroll & Graf, 1998.

Marrs, Jim. *Crossfire: The Plot That Killed Kennedy*. New York: Carroll & Graf, 1988.

Meagher, Sylvia. *Accessories after the Fact: The Warren Commission, the Authorities and the Report*. New York: Random House, 1967.

Melanson, Phillip S. *Spy Saga: Lee Harvey Oswald and U.S. Intelligence*. New York: Praeger, 1990.

Menninger, Bonar. *Mortal Error: The Shot That Killed JFK*. New York: St. Martin's Press, 1992.

Morrow, Robert. *First Hand Knowledge: How I Participated in the CIA-Mafia Murder of JFK*. New York: Sure Seller, 1992.

National Insecurity Council Staff. *It's a Conspiracy*. Oregon: Earth Works, 1992.

Newman, John. *JFK and Vietnam: Deception, Intrigue, and the Struggle for Power*. New York, Warner Books, 1992.

*The Official Warren Commission Report on the Assassination of President John F. Kennedy*. New York: Doubleday, 1964.

Oglesby, Carl. *The JFK Assassination: The Facts and the Theories*. New York: Signet, 1992.

Oglesby, Carl. *Who Killed JFK?* New York: Signet, 1992.

Posner, Gerald. *Case Closed: Lee Harvey Oswald and the Assassination of JFK.* New York: Random House, 1993.

Prouty, L. Fletcher. *JFK: CIA, Vietnam, and the Plot to Assassinate John F. Kennedy.* New York: Citadel Press, 1996.

Roffman, Howard. *Presumed Guilty.* New York: Barnes, 1976.

Russell, Dick. *The Man Who Knew Too Much.* New York: Carroll & Graf, 1992.

Schotz, E. Martin. *History Will Not Absolve Us: Orwellian Control, Public Denial and the Murder of President Kennedy.* Brookline, MA: Kurtz, Ulmer, DeLucia, 1996.

Scott, Peter Dale. *Deep Politics and the Death of JFK.* Berkeley: University of California Press, 1993.

Smith, Matthew. *JFK: The Second Plot.* Edinburgh, Scotland: Main Stream, 1992.

Summers, Anthony. *Conspiracy.* New York: Paragon House, 1989.

Thomas, Kenn, and Lincoln Lawrence. *Mind Control, Oswald and JFK.* Kempton, IL: Adventures Unlimited Press, 1997.

Torbitt, William. *NASA, Nazis and JFK: The Torbitt Document and the JFK Assassination.* Kempton, IL: Adventures Unlimited Press, 1996.

Twyman, Noel. *Bloody Treason: The Assassination of John F. Kennedy.* Rancho Santa Fe, CA: Laurel Publishing, 1997.

Weberman, Alan J., with Michael Canfield. *Coup D'Etat in America: The CIA and the Assassination of John F. Kennedy.* San Francisco: Quick American Publishing, 1975.

Weisberg, Harold. *Case Open: The Unanswered Questions.* New York: Carroll & Graf, 1994.

**Audiotapes**

*JFK: Conspiracy.* Narrated by Edwin Newman. Los Angeles: Audio Renaissance Tapes, 1990.

**Videotapes**

*Beyond JFK: The Question of Conspiracy.* Produced by Danny Schechter and Rori O'Connor. Embassy International Pictures, 1992.

## Other Stuff

Brancato, Paul, and Bill Sienkiewicz. *Coup D'Etat, The Assassination of John F. Kennedy Trading Cards.* Forestville, CA: Eclipse Enterprises, 1990.

## UFOs, Etc.

Bramley, William. *The Gods of Eden.* New York: Avon, 1993.

Evans, Hilary, and Dennis Stacy, eds. *Fortean Times Presents UFO, 1947–1997, Fifty Years of Flying Saucers.* London: John Brown, 1997.

Good, Timothy. *Above Top Secret: The Worldwide UFO Cover-up.* New York: Quill Paperbacks, 1989.

Johnson, DeWayne B., and Kenn Thomas. *Flying Saucers Over Los Angeles: The UFO Craze of the 50s.* Kempton, IL: Adventures Unlimited Press, 1998.

Keith, Jim. *Black Helicopters II, The End Game Strategy.* Lilburn, GA: IllumiNet Press, 1997.

Keith, Jim. *Casebook on the Men in Black.* Lilburn, GA: IllumiNet Press, 1997.

Lyne, William R. *Space Aliens from the Pentagon: Flying Saucers Are Man-Made Electrical Machines.* Lamy, NM: Creatopia Productions, 1995.

Marrs, Jim. *Alien Agenda, Investigating the Extraterrestrial Presence among Us.* New York: Harper Collins, 1997.

## Catalogs

Adventures Unlimited
One Adventure Place
P.O. Box 74
Kempton, IL 60946

Arcturus Books Inc.
1443 S.E. Port St. Lucie Blvd.
Port St. Lucie, FL 34952

Flatland Press
P.O. Box 2420
Ft. Bragg, CA 95437-2420

The Last Hurrah Bookshop
849 West Third Street #1
Williamsport, PA 17701

## Magazines

Prevailing Winds Magazine
P.O. Box 23511
Santa Barbara, CA 93121

Steamshovel Press
P.O. Box 23715
St. Louis, MO 63121

UFO Magazine
8123 Foothill Boulevard
Sunland, CA 91040

# Index

Armstrong, Neil, 177, 179, 181, 182
Arnold, Kenneth, 153, 168, 190, 191
Arvad, Inga, 132–33
*Assassination Films, The,* 18
Assassin profile, 123

Babushka Lady, 19, 106
Baker, Marrion, 74
Balsiger, David, 93
Bell, Aubrey, 26
Bernstein, Carl, 113, 114–15
Binder, Otto, 182
Boas, Antonio Villas, 210–11
Boggs, T. Hale, 31, 32
Boone, Eugene, 58
Booth, John Wilkes, 92, 93–94
Bossa, E. C., 163
Boyd, James William, 94
Brazel, Mac, 155–56, 159
Brennan, Howard, 15, 37, 38, 39, 64
Brown, Madeline, 86
Burkley, George G., 35
Bush, George, 1–2

Chatelain, Maurice, 182–83
Cheramie, Rose, 100
Childress, David Hatcher, 183, 184
CIA, 10, 50, 78, 79, 80, 83, 100, 113–19,
    136, 183
Clinton, Bill, 31
Connally, John, 10, 26, 27, 53, 75
Conspiracy theory, 1–3
Cooper, Gordon, 138
Cooper, John Sherman, 32
Craig, Roger, 56, 58
Creighton, Gordon, 172
Crisman, Fred, 191
Crowe, William D., 106
Cuban exiles, and Kennedy assassination,
    79–80
Curry, Jesse, 46
Cutler, Robert, 22

Dahl, Harold, 190–91
David, Jay, 63
DeMohrenschildt, George, 101

Donahue, Howard, 62
Dulles, Allen, 31

Extraterrestrials. *See* UFOs and extraterrestrials

FBI, 10–11, 73, 101, 107, 115, 132, 133
Federal Emergency Management Agency (FEMA), 199–200
Fetzer, James H., 18
Ford, Gerald, 25, 27, 31–32, 73, 75, 91
Frazier, Robert, 63

Garrison, Jim, 35
Giancana, Sam, 100, 106
Goldwater, Barry, 154, 156
Good, Timothy, 167, 182
Greer, Steven, 141
Greer, William, 46
Groden, Robert, 14, 121

Hall, Manly P., 188
Helicopters, black, 195–200
Hepburn, James, 5
Hickey, George, 46
Hill, Clint, 18, 46
Hillenkoetter, Roscoe, 138
Hitler, Adolf, 132, 139, 167, 169
Hoagland, Richard, 183, 202–3, 205–6
Hoffman, Ed, 41
Hoover, J. Edgar, 68, 81, 83, 111, 129–34
Hughes, Robert, 17
Hume, J. J., 35
Humes, James, 122
Hynek, J. Allen, 158

*JFK,* 115, 128, 148
Johnson, Lyndon, 25, 29–30, 56, 81, 85–86, 88

Kammler, Ernst, 145–46
Kasher, Jack, 184
Kaysing, Bill, 177–79, 180
Keel, John, 168
Keith, Jim, 188, 189, 197, 199
Kennedy, John F.
  Hoover's file on, 132–33
  UFO knowledge of, 136, 216–17

Kennedy assassination
  autopsy in, 95–97, 100–101, 121–23
  bullet holes in clothing, 64–65
  bullets in, 26, 35, 53
  death of witnesses, 99–101
  FBI report on, 10–11
  and film evidence, 17, 57
    doctoring of, 18
    suppression of, 19
    Zapruder film, 13–15, 18, 21, 61, 116
  hearing about, 9–10
  -Lincoln assassination parallel, 92, 93
  Manchurian Candidate scenario, 31
  and media, 115, 118–19
  and motorcade route, 45–46, 111
  previous known attempts, 10
  Secret Service behavior during, 45–47
  single-bullet theory, 25–27, 32, 34, 61–65
  sniper's nest area, 55–57
  suicide theory of, 89
  suspects in, 77–83, 85–89, 134, 215–16
  UFO theory, 189
  Umbrella Man–as–shooter theory, 21–23
  weapons-carrying bystanders at, 43–44
  See also Oswald, Lee Harvey; Warren Commission
Kennedy, Robert, 77, 80, 131
Kerry, John, 45
KGB, and Kennedy assassination, 81–82
Kilgallen, Dorothy, 109–11, 162

Latona, Sebastian, 57
Lawrence, Lincoln, 76
Lifton, David, 96
Lincoln assassination, 92, 93–94
Little, Gregory, 211, 212
Livingstone, Harrison Edward, 18, 96, 121

McCloy, John J., 31
Mafia, 80–81, 100, 106, 131, 134
Marcel, Jesse, 156
Markham, Helen, 37, 38, 39, 64
Marrs, Jim, 127–28
  on Kennedy assassination, 38–39, 46, 101, 106–7, 131
  on UFOs, 136, 137, 140–49, 150, 157, 168, 175, 184, 189, 198, 202, 216
Mars probe, 201–8

Media, CIA influence on, 113–19
Men in Black (MIB), 187–93
Menninger, Bonar, 46
Mercer, Julia Ann, 104
Meyer, Mary, 100
Milam, Wallace, 56
Milteer, Joseph, 10
Moon landings, 3, 177–86
Muchmore, Mary, 17

NASA, 177–85, 186, 201–8
Nazis
    flying disk research of, 145–46, 167, 168
    in U.S., 31, 78, 166
*New York Times*, 114–15, 118
Nix, Orville, 17, 18
Nixon, Richard, 87, 88–89, 106, 130

Oberg, James, 179
Oliver, Beverly, 19, 106
O'Neil, Francis X., 35
Oswald, Lee Harvey
    background of, 49–52
    "backyard photo" of, 69
    evidence against, 52–53, 56–57, 74
    government links to, 10, 50, 73, 78
    and imposter theory, 67–71
    killing of, 2, 5–6, 11, 39, 103–7, 110
    mafia links to, 39, 81
    marksmanship of, 34, 51, 61–62, 64
    motives of, 74–76
    and murder weapon, 26, 52–53, 56–57, 58, 63
    palm print of, 57, 59
    Ruby's links to, 106–7
    and Tippit murder, 39, 51–52, 69, 74, 111
Oswald, Marguerite, 67–68, 103
Oswald, Marina, 35, 37–38, 39, 64, 75

Pendleton, Revilo, 34
Peterson, Viola, 34
Pitzer, William, 100–101
Posner, Gerald, 61–62, 63–65
Presidential assassinations, 91–94
    *See also* Kennedy assassination
Presley, Elvis, 1, 2

Ramirez, Manuel Angel, 189
Rather, Dan, 116–17, 118

Reagan, Ronald, 153
Redlich, Norman, 34, 35
Rivell, Richard, 71
Roselli, Johnny, 100, 106
Roswell (New Mexico), 156–59, 162–63, 190, 216
Ruby, Jack, 11, 39, 81, 88–89, 96, 100, 101, 103–7, 110
Rushing, Roy, 104
Russell, Richard, 32

Secret Service, 18, 45–47, 89, 123
Seibert, James W., 35
Sellier, Charles E., 93
Similas, Norman, 17
Simmons, Ronald, 63
Somersett, William M., 10
Spector, Arlen, 34
Spencer, Saundra, 122
Stone, Oliver, 115, 128, 148–49
Stringfield, Leonard H., 163
Summers, Anthony, 130–31, 133

Tilson, Tom, 104
Tippit, J. D., 38–39, 51–52, 69, 74, 110, 111
Tolson, Clyde, 131, 134
Truly, Roy, 74
Truman, Harry, 142, 161
Twining, Nathan, 138
Twyman, Noel, 18, 64

UFOs and extraterrestrials
    abductions by, 141, 142, 145, 148, 172–74
    black helicopters, 195–200
    crash sites, 161–64, 216
    human origins theory of, 165–69
    Kennedy's knowledge of, 136, 216–17
    on Mars, 201–8
    Men in Black (MIB), 187–93
    on moon, 181–86
    motives and plans of, 171–72, 175
    myths about, 139–50
    physical appearance of, 163, 174
    possibility for, 135–38
    sexual congress with, 209–14
    shapes of, 155
    sightings and encounters, 153–59, 185
Umbrella Man, 21–23

Vallee, Thomas Arthur, 10
Vankin, Jonathan, 118
Vidal, Gore, 3
Von Braun, Werner, 145–46

Wallace, Malcolm, 56
Walthers, Buddy, 100
Warren, Earl, 29, 30, 32
Warren Commission, 2, 3, 14, 55, 57, 58, 74, 96
   conclusions of, 33–35
     failure to call witnesses, 35

   and LBJ's motives, 29–30
   members of, 25, 30–32
   witnesses before, 37–40
Weisberg, Harold, 74
Weitzman, Seymour, 58
Whalen, John, 118
White, Jack, 70
White, Roscoe, 69
Witt, Louis Steven, 23

Zapruder film, 13–15, 18, 21, 61, 116

About the Author

RICHARD BELZER, the veteran stand-up comic, actor, talk show host, and author was born in Bridgeport, Connecticut. Thrown out of, or asked politely to leave, every school he ever attended "due to uncontrollable wit," Belzer parlayed his talent outside of the classroom into a career that has spanned two decades.

For the past seven seasons Richard Belzer starred as Detective John Munch on the Peabody Award–winning NBC series *Homicide: Life on the Street*. Within forty-eight hours of *Homicide*'s recent cancellation, a deal was struck with *Law & Order* creator Dick Wolf to transfer Munch from Baltimore to New York, where he is taking up residence on *Law & Order: Special Victims Unit*, NBC's new spin-off of *Law & Order*.

Widely known for his astute political observations and an insatiable appetite for the news, Belzer began his career as a reporter for the *Bridgeport Post* and several other newspapers around the country. This interest can be traced directly back to his days as a paperboy in his hometown. Belzer honed his life experiences into barbed comedic material drawn from former jobs as a teacher, census taker, jewelry salesman, dock worker, and several other unmentionable occupations.

Richard Belzer began his career in show business with a starring role in *Groove Tube*, the counterculture film that went on to become a cult classic. Since then, Belzer's comedic talents have been featured in every show business medium from off-Broadway (*The National Lampoon Show* with Bill Murray, Gilda Radner, and John Belushi) to radio (*Brink and Belzer* morning drive-time WNBC) to major Hollywood movies (*Fame*; *Author, Author*; *Night Shift*; and *Scarface*).

For the small screen, Belzer recently made television history when his *Homicide* character, Detective John Munch, appeared in three different prime-time series in the same week (*Homicide*, *Law & Order*, and *The X-Files*). With the addition of Munch to *Law & Order: Special Victims Unit* and an upcoming Munch appearance on Tom Fontana and Barry Levinson's new series *The Beat*, Belzer will set another record: the first time in history the same character has appeared on five different prime-time series.

Belzer starred in his own comedy special for HBO entitled "Another Lone Nut"; the hour-long special was a mix of vintage "Belzer" and topical material culled from the state of today's political climate. He hosted Comedy Central's 1997 year-end "Town Meeting" special, and he recently hosted an ABC prime-time special "When Cars Attack." He also appeared in "Elmopalooza," ABC's prime-time special commemorating *Sesame Street*'s thirtieth anniversary. Belzer's first-ever comedy CD, *Another Lone Nut,* was recently released by Uproar Records.

Belzer has made numerous appearances on *Saturday Night Live*, *The Tonight Show*, and *Late Night with David Letterman*, was a regular on *Thicke of the Night*, and had his own six-part comedy series, *The Richard Belzer Show,* directed for Cinemax by David Steinberg. He hosted the live national talk show *Hot Properties* on the Lifetime Cable Network. In addition, Richard Belzer is the author of *How to Be a Stand-up Comic*, published by Random House, a satirical book with practical information for today's would-be comics.

Upcoming projects include an animated series for Nelvana, *Belzer's Conspiracy Chronicles* (featuring a cartoon Belzer hosting) and a feature-length documentary following Richard on his national book tour promoting *UFOs, JFK, and Elvis*.

Belzer's comedy is perceptive and unrestrained by conventions, emanating from a free thinker who has no reservations about saying what is on his mind; that has become Belzer's legendary trademark. There's as much spontaneous invention in a Belzer performance as there are set pieces. The audience never knows what he'll do next . . . and neither does he. It's comedy with an edge, laughter with a thrill.

Richard Belzer and his actress wife, Harlee McBride, have two daughters, Jessica and Bree. They live in New York while filming *Law & Order: Special Victims Unit* and in France during the rest of the year.